Orphans

TONBRIDGE SCHOOL LIBRARY

Remember to check your books out on the computer.
Stamp this label with the date for return.

- 3 JUL 2006

This Film is dedicated to
Patricia Mullan
1923–93

Introduction

I first saw *Orphans* at the Edinburgh Film Festival in the summer of 1998. I had high hopes for the film because I knew its director, Peter Mullan, to be a very sussed-out man, extremely passionate about what he does. I originally met him on the set of *Trainspotting* and I later saw his short film *Fridge*, which impressed me enough to ask him if he felt like directing one of a series of short films I was planning to screenwrite. Peter declined, explaining that he had some ideas of his own which he was keen to develop. This turned out to be good judgement on his part in the light of what he was subsequently to produce.

What he was developing at the time was *Orphans*, his first feature as a writer-director. At the same time, he was taking the lead part in Ken Loach's film *My Name is Joe* and going on, among other things, to deservedly win the Best Actor Award at the Cannes Film Festival. So it wasn't a bad year for him!

Orphans more than met my expectations, to the extent that I consider it to be one of the finest films ever to have come out of Britain, a film destined for classic status. It's certainly one of the few British movies I'll watch again and again. Even if it does spectacularly well at the box office, it probably still won't get the audience it deserves. The machinations of the British film industry are such that it's a small miracle any movies are made at all, let alone ever screened. It isn't the easiest of films to promote and market, particularly for an industry which, despite occasional hype to the contrary and the odd notable exception, is not really characterized by high levels of innovation and risk-taking.

As a film *Orphans* certainly has three qualities, even though the title conjures up an image of poor wee bairns left all alone in the world. In fact, as it opens we find that the grown-up Flynn siblings, Thomas (Gary Lewis), Michael (Douglas Henshall), John (Stephen McCole) and Sheila (Rosemarie Stevenson), have just lost their mother, and their father is long gone.

The power of the film lies in how the script handles the universal but almost taboo issue of bereavement, with its attendant overwhelming feelings of guilt, anger, resentment and denial, all set in a working-class Scottish cultural context. Thomas, the oldest brother, has lost himself in religion, pretending to consider but actually neglecting the needs of the wheelchair-bound Sheila. Michael, on the other hand, sees the opportunity to work a scam as a way of providing a focus through his forest of confusion. John teams up with petty crook Tanga and has some displaced form of violent revenge on his agenda.

The irreverent and subversive power of the script is fuelled by brave directing and tremendous acting performances. There are some intensely memorable scenes, particularly where the baddest bastard of a barman ever (Alex Norton) gets his comeuppance and the fantastic emotional pay-off when Michael gives the heart-rending speech to his bemused workmates about how he wants compensation. The horrendous yet paradoxically people-affirming realization is that there can be no compensation – all there was was his mammy.

Anybody who has ever experienced the (hopefully temporary) insanity that is bereavement will be able to laugh and cry along with this ground-breaking movie, and will find it harrowing and uplifting at the same time. It's also a must-see for those of us who marvel at superb acting performances. Gary Lewis and Stephen McCole are brilliant in their respective denial and anger, while Douglas Henshall is incandescent, his hurt and rage and confusion burning through the screen. And it's just impossible to believe that Rosemarie Stevenson had never acted prior to this film.

When you come out of the cinema after *Orphans*, you feel that you have seen both a very important and a very entertaining movie. That's the upside. On the downside, you feel that it's going to be a while before you see anything quite as significant again. And when all's said and done, you can't really ask for much more from a film, can you?

Irvine Welsh, *March 1999*

Orphans

INT. KITCHEN. LATE AFTERNOON. PRESENT DAY

Coffee, milk, sugar, tea, biscuits, ashtrays, cigarette packets and lighters are all strewn across the kitchen table, around which are sat Michael, Thomas, Sheila, John, Aunt Geraldine and Uncle Ian. They are all laughing hysterically as Uncle Ian is high-flying through one of his many anecdotes.

UNCLE IAN

Every time the gaffer came over we aw started miming.
(*mouths something*)
An' he's aw, 'Christ, Ah just bought this hearing aid an' it's bloody useless.' So Ah says, 'Maybe it's no' the hearing aid, maybe it's the batteries.' So he goes oot at lunchtime an' buys a new set of batteries. He comes up tae me an' says, 'Hey, Ian, say somethin'.' Ah says, 'Whit dae ye want me tae say?' 'Aw, that's aw right,' he says, 'Ah heard that. It must have been the batteries right enough.'

The doorbell goes. Thomas gets up and goes to answer it. Uncle Ian continues.

Ah says, 'There, Ah telt ye it wis the . . .
(*mouths*)
Ye should always get the long . . .
(*mouths*)
wans. Save yersel some . . .'
(*mouths*)
'Aw, God,' he says, 'it's breakin' up again . . .'

Howls of laughter from his audience. Thomas comes to the doorway.

THOMAS

Mum's here.

The laughter stops dead. Michael and John get up immediately, followed by Uncle Ian. Sheila presses the button on the side of her wheelchair and goes out into the hallway after them. Aunt Geraldine starts putting cups into the sink.

Thomas comes through the door backwards. As he shuffles in, we see he is carrying the bottom end of a dark wooden coffin. At either side are John and Michael. The undertaker, Mr Leitch, is at the top end. He is followed by his assistant, who carries the trestles. They go into the sitting room.

Sheila watches all this and becomes more and more distressed. John is first out of the sitting room. He looks to Sheila and begins to weep. Sheila, despite her condition, opens her arms and beckons him. Like a little child, he rushes over to her and, on his knees, hugs her. Michael comes out and, crying uncontrollably, does likewise. Thomas comes out and, though more in control, joins his brothers and sisters, wrapping his arms around them.

The front door has remained open and a small crowd of people are looking in, in that slightly insensitive and morbid way that people do. The undertakers leave, ushered out by Uncle Ian, who closes the door firmly. With due respect to his niece's and nephews' grief, he walks back down the hall into the kitchen. We are tracking ahead of him so that when he closes the kitchen door he cuts us off from the family, leaving us to look at a plate hung on the back of the door which has a picture in the middle of Thomas, Michael, Sheila and John surrounding their mother proudly. On the table in front of them is a cake which reads 'Happy Birthday, Mum'. On the wall behind them is a banner which reads 'Young at Sixty'.

INT. BEDROOM. DAY

Michael, Sheila and John are sat by the window. Thomas has a brown cardboard box which is half full of his mother's personal belongings – watches, earrings, brooches, necklaces, rosary beads, etc. He takes out a gold-plated watch and holds it up to the others. They take their gaze momentarily off the empty bed and nod. Thomas puts the watch in his pocket and hands the box to

4

Michael. Michael looks inside and takes out a pair of earrings. He holds the box for Sheila to look into.

Sheila brings out a set of rosary beads. John takes the box from Michael and chooses a brooch.

We have been panning slowly on to each character as they choose their personal memento and each stares at the bed having done so, lost in thought. We continue to pan round the walls of the bedroom and, just as John has gone out of shot and we move along the bedroom wall, day turns to night. We hear thunder and the paintings on the wall light up from flashes of lightning. Still we pan around slowly till we arrive on the bed, where we see a young Thomas (aged thirteen), Michael (aged eight), Sheila (aged ten) and baby John in the arms of his mother, who lies in the middle of them. With every flash and roll of thunder the children flinch and move closer to their mother, who gently reassures them.

MOTHER

It'll pass, don't worry. It'll pass.

Still we pan ever so slowly till we are off the bed and on to the other wall. Midway along, night turns to day and the sound of thunder disappears. Finally, having turned 360 degrees, we are back to our family as they are now, staring at the empty bed. After a few moments Thomas closes the curtains behind them. Above their darkened faces comes the title: ORPHANS.

INT. SITTING ROOM. DAY

The curtains have been drawn. On a table by the coffin there is a battered statuette of the Sacred Heart, flanked by two red candles and a pair of scissors. Thomas picks up the scissors and hands them to Michael.

MICHAEL

What are these for?

THOMAS

You cut a piece of your hair and lay it in the coffin.

MICHAEL

Why?

THOMAS

So there's a part of us in there wi' our mother. We done it at Dad's.

MICHAEL

Ah don't remember.

THOMAS

We did.

(*pause*)

You don't have to if you don't want to. Ah just think it's a good thing to do. Says we're still a family – even after death.

Michael thinks for a moment, then proceeds to cut a small piece of hair from his head and put it in the coffin beside his mother. He hands the scissors to John, who does likewise. He then cuts some of Sheila's hair and puts it in the coffin. He offers the scissors to Uncle Ian and Aunt Geraldine, but they politely refuse. He then hands the scissors back to Thomas, who, with great gravitas, cuts an absurdly large chunk from his forehead, leaving him with a large bald patch. This one-upmanship does not go unnoticed, though nothing is said. Sheila breaks the silence. As she suffers from cerebral palsy, every word involves great physical effort.

SHEILA

I want to kiss Mum goodbye.

The brothers help her out of her wheelchair and hold her precariously over the coffin. Sheila's head trembles involuntarily as her lips meet her mother's.

EXT. OUTSIDE THE CHAPEL. DAY

Thomas, Michael, John, Ian and two other relatives stand with the

coffin resting on their shoulders. The undertaker quietly issues
instructions.

> UNDERTAKER
>
> Now, gentlemen, it's best to take short steps at an even, steady pace. Try not to push up with your shoulders as this will affect the balance.

The priest comes to the side door and gives a nod to the
undertaker.

> UNDERTAKER
>
> All right, gentlemen, we may go in.

The men bolt forward in a decidedly unsteady and unceremonious
manner.

INT. CHAPEL. DAY

The chapel is empty apart from the family, who are seated in the
front row. The priest is saying mass. Thomas is rubbing his
shoulder.

> THOMAS
>
> Ah've definitely pulled a muscle. Bloody agony.

The family ignore him. He looks to John, who's a few seats across.

> THOMAS
>
> John. John!

John glares at him.

> THOMAS
>
> Dae ye know if there's any Ralgex back at our mother's? Eh? John, Ah'm talkin' tae you.

> JOHN
>
> Naw, Ah don't, aw right?

Thomas sits back, then rubs his shoulder again.

                              THOMAS
                        (*almost to himself*)
        Man, it's bloody sore.

*We pan up from the priest to a beautiful, ornate Madonna, who
looks down on them all.*

INT. PUB. NIGHT

*It's band night and the large lounge bar is full of people of all ages.
Michael, John, Thomas and Sheila are seated at a table in the
corner. They don't talk, but just stare out at what's going on
around them: namely, life in all its weird, glorious, sad, happy
complexity.*

*The leader of the band announces that Frank has just become a
daddy and is going to come up on the stage and give them a song.
Frank, drunk but good-natured, jumps onstage and belts into a
version of 'Isn't She Lovely?'.*

*We see the pub from different points of view. Michael concentrates
on Frank's sweaty, happy face, trying hard to remember what it
felt like when he was first a father. John notices Duncan and his
mates slipping a joint under the table and laughing hysterically.
Sheila hones in on an elderly lady roughly the same age as her
mother singing along to the song. Thomas looks at the band
strumming along, calling the tune but distant from all that goes on
around them. The song finishes to huge applause.*

INT. TOILET. NIGHT

Michael and John stand side by side at the urinal.

                              MICHAEL
        When's the exams?

                               JOHN
        Next week.

MICHAEL

Next week? Fuck, bad timin'. How dae ye think you'll get on?

JOHN

Don't know. Tell ye the truth, don't fuckin' care.

He zips up and leaves. Frank comes in and instantly starts berating a young lad who is putting money into the condom machine.

FRANK

Whit the fuck dae ye want them fir? Get them tae fuck. You want to be a man, you fuckin' get out there an' make babies. Hundreds and hundreds ae babies,
(*turns tae Michael*)

Am Ah right?

MICHAEL)
(*humouring him*)

Aye, ye're right.

FRANK

Ye goat wanes?

MICHAEL

Two.

FRANK
(*to lad*)

See. This cunt's goat two hundred wanes.

He puts his hand around Michael's neck, brings his head to his lips and gives Michael a big kiss on the cheek.

Ah love ye, man. Ah fuckin' love ye.

The lad passes by them.

LAD

Sad auld poofter.

FRANK
(*shouting after him*)
Ye might well be right, young man. Ye might well be right.

Michael zips up and goes, Frank shouting after him
Every cunt should love every cunt. That's what Ah say!

INT. PUB. NIGHT

Michael makes his way to the end of the bar to order drinks from the waitress standing there. He hasn't noticed that Thomas has made his way to the stage, so his order is halted when he hears his brother's voice booming clumsily through the microphone.

THOMAS
Ah'd like to dedicate this song to my mother . . .

There are a few humorous 'aaah's from the audience.

. . . who sadly died from a heart attack day before yesterday. The funeral service is in Holy Cross Church tomorrow at ten o'clock. So anyone who wants to come along is more than welcome.

The bar is stunned into almost total silence. The band is equally gobsmacked.

A-one, a-two, a-one, two, three, four . . .

As he begins his song, 'The Air That I Breathe', Michael looks across at John. The two of them can't help but quietly laugh at all this. The waitress waves her pen under his nose.

WAITRESS
Hey, you! The man's just lost his mother, so get that stupid smile aff yer face. And that goes for you lot inaw.

She glares at Duncan, who, together with his friends, is in tears laughing. Michael stares at them also. The waitress speaks to him.

Noo, you wantin' bottled Coke wi' yer vodka?

MICHAEL
(*still looking at Duncan*)

Aye.

WAITRESS

Where ye sittin'?

MICHAEL

Over there.

WAITRESS

Right, Ah'll bring them o'er.

She turns towards the bar, shouting the order to the bar staff.
Michael stays put. He can't take his eyes off Duncan. The more
Duncan laughs, the colder this sudden rage within him becomes.

Thomas begins to break down. He tries to carry on singing but
can't Sheila and John can only look on helplessly. The band grinds
to an embarrassed halt. Thomas stands there, head bowed,
mumbling . . .

THOMAS

I'm sorry. I'm sorry. I'm sorry. I'm . . .

Suddenly there is a scream. A table is turned over and people jump
out of the way as three or four men lash out. John looks across
and sees that Michael is at the centre of it. He has Duncan by the
hair and is kicking his face while dragging him to the door. The
bouncers come in and start separating. John runs across and
punches one of Duncan's mates. Three or four other men join in
and the whole mêlée bursts out through the doors. Somewhere in
all this Frank gets involved, shouting about how we should all love
one another. He is punched in the mouth for his troubles.

Sheila tries to move her wheelchair from behind the table but she
can't negotiate it by herself. With great effort she shouts.

SHEILA

Thomas!

Thomas remains where he is, head bowed, muttering. Sheila jerks out an arm, which sends the glasses flying off the table. And her wheelchair just keeps banging against the table.

EXT. PUB. NIGHT

Duncan, his brother Lenny and Mona are thrown out of the pub by the bouncers. Mona, shouts at them.

> MONA
> Whit we gettin' flung oot fir? That cunt started it.

> DUNCAN
> Mona, c'mon.

> MONA
> Bunch ah pricks!
> > *(to Duncan)*
> He should be gettin' flung oot, no' us.

Duncan grabs her.

> DUNCAN
> Move!

They walk away.

> LENNY
> Whit ye daen? We should be hangin' aboot tae fuckin' kill they cunts.

> DUNCAN
> > *(under his breath)*
> Ah goat him, aw right?

> LENNY
> Whit?

> DUNCAN
> Check this.

Duncan stands under a streetlight. Looking over his shoulder, he

shows Mona a knife which has blood on it. Frank, who has also been thrown out, looks to the bouncers.

> FRANK
>
> Whit did Ah dae? Aw Ah said wis we should aw love one another.

> BOUNCER
> *(with no hint of irony)*
>
> No' the night, pal.

He slams the glass door shut. Frank can only stare in disbelief.

INT. PUB TOILET. NIGHT

Michael stands in the cubicle looking incredulously at the blood seeping out of his belly. He rolls up his shirt and we see a small stab wound. He starts unrolling toilet paper and pressing it against the wound.

INT. PUB. NIGHT

Michael comes out of the toilet, his arms carefully placed in front of him. He joins Sheila, John and Thomas at the table.

> MICHAEL
>
> Ah'm gonny have tae go.

> JOHN
>
> Ah'll come wi' ye.

> MICHAEL
>
> Thomas, you get Sheila up the road, aw right?

Thomas nods.

> SHEILA
>
> Don't go, Michael.

Michael kisses her.

MICHAEL

It's aw right, Sheila. Ah'm no gaun tae fight. Ah promise.
Ah lost it for a wee bit there but I'm aw right noo. Nae
mare fightin', Ah swear. Ah'll see ye back at the house. Ah
love ye.

*Michael goes, followed by John. Sheila watches them go, then
notices blood on the arm of her wheelchair. Thomas lifts Sheila's
drink to her mouth, but she shakes her head and begins rocking
from side to side in sheer frustration at her powerlessness. The
band strike up 'Let's Dance'.*

EXT. OUTSIDE PUB. NIGHT

JOHN

He whit?

MICHAEL

Cunt stabbed me.

JOHN

Ah'm gonny kill that greasy bastard. Ah'm gonny fuckin' . . .
We better get you tae casualty.

He runs out and stops a taxi. They get in.

Vicki Infirmary please, mate.

The taxi driver turns and looks at Michael.

DRIVER

Whit's up wi' him?

MICHAEL

Him's no feelin' good.

DRIVER

You bleedin'? You'll have tae get oot, pal, coz Ah canny have
ye bleedin' aw oer mah seats.

MICHAEL

Whit if Ah opened the windae an' bled out there? Wid that be
aw right?

DRIVER

Sorry, pal, you'll need tae get oot. This isnae mah cab. Ah only
dae the back shift. Ah canny have blood oan the seats.

JOHN

Just take us tae the fuckin' hospital!

DRIVER

Sorry, Ah canny have blood oan the seats.
(*to John*)
An' yer no allowed tae smoke in the cab.

John throws his cigarette at the glass window.

JOHN

Stick yer fuckin' cab!

*He opens the door and gets out. Michael stares at the driver for a
few moments, then gets out of the taxi. The taxi drives off.*

INT. PUB. NIGHT

Thomas is talking to a sympathetic-looking old lady.

THOMAS

I just pictured her lying there all alone in the church and
suddenly my heart just . . . It was one of her favourite songs
as well. She also liked Patsy Cline, but I thought she might be
a bit morbid.

*Sheila leans forward to drink from her glass, but her mouth pushes
too hard on the straw and the glass tumbles. Thomas turns to her.*

It's all right, Sheila. It's all right.
(*he shouts to the waitress*)
Excuse me, could we have a cloth please? Thank you. It's all
right, Sheila. I'll wipe it up and get you another drink.

OLD LADY

Do you live with your sister?

THOMAS

Aye. Now that mah mother's gone I'm kind of Sheila's guardian, or whatever it's called. Carer. I was glad I was able to tell my mother that before she died. I think she went more peacefully, knowing that Sheila would be looked after.

OLD LADY

Ah'm sure she did. That's very good of ye. It's no easy job. Ah cared fir mah own mother for nearly twenty years.

THOMAS

Twenty years, my God. When did she die?

OLD LADY

Aw, she's no deid. Naw, she's in a home now. Ah couldnae really manage any more.

Thomas glares at her, stunned for the moment. The waitress puts the cloth on the table. Thomas ignores it.

THOMAS

What age is your mother?

OLD LADY

Ninety-two, an' still sharp as a tack. But her legs an' her bowels have gone, y'know.

She notices that Thomas's attitude has changed dramatically as he stares at her with near open contempt.

What age was your mother?

Thomas ignores her, wipes the table, then leaves to go to the bar.

SHEILA

She   was   seventy   one.

OLD LADY

Sorry, dear, Ah didnae quite hear that.

Sheila shakes her head. She can't be bothered repeating it.

EXT. STREET. NIGHT

Michael and John are walking.

JOHN

Where ur we gaun?

Michael stops outside Evette's Massage Parlour. He raps the door.

Whit? Ye gaun fir a shag?

MICHAEL

Margaret's a nurse.

JOHN

Who the fuck's Margaret?

MICHAEL

A friend. Right, ye comin' in?

JOHN

Ah'm no gaun in there. Fuck.

MICHAEL

Well, wait oot here fir us.

JOHN

Ah'm no waitin' out here. Everybody thinkin' Ah'm a sad cunt. Ah'll see ye up the corner.

The door opens. Michael is ushered in by Maria, the receptionist, who is extremely pretty. John is surprised.

You the nurse?

Maria smiles, then speaks through gritted teeth.

                              MARIA
Do I look like a fucking nurse?

She slams the door in his face.

                              JOHN
Ah just asked, for fuck's sake.

He walks away.

INT. MARGARET'S CUBICLE/ROOM. NIGHT

*Michael sits on the edge of the 'massage' table while Margaret
tends to the wound. She tears a long strip of Elastoplast.*

                            MICHAEL
Naw, don't use that. Ah don't want anything that'll leave a
mark.

                            MARGARET
Why?

                            MICHAEL
Ah'm gonny go into work the morra, make out it happened
there. That ways Ah can claim industrial injury.

                            MARGARET.
They'll no' buy that.

                            MICHAEL
Charlie McGuire broke his arm at the fitba'. He waited till
Monday mornin', went intae his work, lay doon on the floor
an' started yellin'. He goat nearly ten grand in compensation.

                            MARGARET
That was a broken arm, Mick. This is a stab wound. Ye could
lose a lot of blood by the mornin'.

                            MICHAEL
It's no' that bad, is it?

MARGARET

Ye've goat tae get tae the hospital. There could be all sorts ah complications.

MICHAEL

Naw, fuck it, Ah need the money.

MARGARET

Ah don't think it's worth bleedin' tae death.

MICHAEL

Listen, Ah've got two kids and a wife that's divorcin' me. Believe me, Ah'm already bleedin' tae fuckin' death. Ah'll be aw right. Noo, just wrap a bandage round that, wid ye?

EXT. STREET CORNER. NIGHT

John is about to light a cigarette. An old yellow Vauxhall Viva goes screaming past, swerving into a large, deep puddle as it does, sending a wave of black water over the unsuspecting John. For a moment he just stands there, frozen to the spot, his cigarette sadly drooping from his mouth. Then he turns and runs like a man possessed after the car.

INT./EXT. CAR (VAUXHALL) AT TRAFFIC LIGHTS. NIGHT

An elderly gentleman sits listening to Radio Four, waiting for the green light. Suddenly a sodden jacket is whacked against the windscreen. John bangs the side of the window.

JOHN
(*screaming*)
See whit ye done tae mah jacket, ya auld bastard? Eh? Dae ye see whit ye done? Ye fuckin' soaked me, ya blind auld prick!

The gentleman just sits, staring ahead, obviously terrified.

Well, whit ye goat tae say fir yersel', eh? Ye deaf as well as blind?

Three young lads (aged about twelve) have been watching this while walking by. Rab speaks up.

RAB

Aw, fuckin' leave the auld guy alane.

An extremely worked-up John looks over to them.

JOHN

Whit did you say? Whit did you say, prick?

RAB

Leave him alone. Pick on someone yer ane size.

JOHN

Aw right, you want tae come ahead then? C'mere! Ah said c'mere.

The lads begin to walk faster. John speaks to the elderly gent.

Don't you fuckin' move. You stay right where you fuckin' are. Right you, c'mere.

He walks rapidly round the front of the car. The lads take off. He runs after them but not very far as he hears the car speed off. He stops, shouting after the car.

Get back here wi' mah jaicket, ya cunt!

He runs back towards the car, but it's well into the distance. He looks around and sees his jacket on the road. Without looking, he steps out to get it. There is a screech as a bus brakes, followed by an instant banging on the horn. The driver pulls back the window and puts his head round.

DRIVER

Whit the fuck you daen, ya crazy bastard!

JOHN

Whit did you call me? Whit did you call me?

DRIVER

Ye nearly goat yersel' killed! Noo get off the fuckin' road!

JOHN

Whit? Think ye're a big shot coz ye're in a bus. Get oot here and we'll see who's the big shot! Just you an' me, c'mon! C'mon!

John starts kicking the bus. Michael approaches him.

MICHAEL

It's a bus, ye daft cunt. You gonny take oan a bus?

Michael pushes him out of the way.

JOHN
(shouting as the bus goes by, passengers
ogling this weird young man)
Any time, big man. Ah'll take ye oan. Ah'll take any one ae yez oan!

MICHAEL

Jesus fuckin' wept, whit is up wi' you? Gonny just calm doon?

JOHN

Ah'll calm doon when Ah see you put a hatchet through that cunt Duncan's heid.

MICHAEL

Man, you talk some pish. Ah'm no puttin' a hatchet through anybody's heid. It wis mah fault. Ah shouldnae have went fir him but ah did. So now Ah just have tae get on wi' it. Wi' a bit of luck the bastard might have done us a favour.

JOHN

Whit ye talking about?

MICHAEL

Industrial injury. If Ah make out it happened at work then Ah could be liable for compensation. Could be worth as much as ten grand.

JOHN

Is that aw you ever think about? Fuckin' money. So whit then?
Ye gonna buy Duncan a box of chocolates?

MICHAEL

No. Flowers.

JOHN

Noo you might no' give a fuck about our family but Ah dae.
That scum stabbed mah brother an' Ah'm gonny get him fir it.

John starts walking away.

MICHAEL

Aye, sure he'll shite himsel' fae you, college boy.

JOHN

Don't you gie me that. Ah only done it fir wur ma. But she's
gone now, isn't she? In't she!

MICHAEL

Aye, she is.

JOHN

Right then. So noo Ah can dae whatever the fuck Ah like! An
who's gonny stop me? Eh? Who?
        (*he begins shouting at the top of his voice*)
Ah'm gonny kill Duncan!

He looks up at the windows and screams at passing cars.

Ah'm gonny kill Duncan!

*Curtains remain closed and motorists drive on. He turns to
Michael.*

See! Nobody gives a fuck. You better get up the road,
Michael. Ah heard there's a storm comin'.

*John marches away. Michael watches him go before turning and
walking off slowly in the other direction.*

24

EXT. CHURCH. NIGHT

The priest is locking the front doors. Thomas approaches with Sheila behind him.

THOMAS

Evenin', Father.

PRIEST

Good evenin' . . . eh . . .

THOMAS

Would you mind if mah sister an' me spent some time inside wi' mah mother?

PRIEST

Ah wis just lockin' up.

THOMAS

Ah'm no being' cheeky, Father, but Ah thought the doors of the church were always open.

PRIEST

There's no' many churches can afford tae dae that any more. Just last week somebody broke in an' stole the chalice.

THOMAS

They stole the chalice? Whit dae ye make ah that, Sheila? They stole the chalice. Wid that no be a huge mortal sin, Father?

PRIEST

All stealin' is a mortal sin.

THOMAS

Ah, but stealin' the chalice. That must be up there wi' murder. Well, that settles it fir me, Father. There's no way Ah'm leavin' mah mother alone in a church when there's people like that runnin' about.

PRIEST

Aye, but your mother's . . .

(*he just manages to stop himself saying 'dead'*)

perfectly safe. We've installed a new alarm system.

THOMAS

Ah worked as a security guard for three years, Father, an', if ye'll excuse mah French, alarm systems urnae worth shite. If ye give me the keys, Father, Ah'll look after the place.

PRIEST

Believe me, Ah would if Ah could, but Ah have tae think about insurance.

THOMAS

Please, Father.

PRIEST

Ah'm sorry. Ah can't. Really, it's just not possible.

There is a long pause as he looks at Thomas and Sheila's imploring faces.

INT. CHURCH. NIGHT

Thomas locks the door.

PRIEST

And don't forget the side door!

THOMAS

Ah won't, Father. Ye can trust me.

He and Sheila go inside the church. They go slowly down the aisle and stop in front of the coffin. Thomas speaks with near-comic gravitas.

We're here for ye, Ma. I, Thomas, yer eldest son, is here. So too is Sheila, second eldest and only daughter. Your other sons, Michael and John, got intae a fight in a pub an' we don't know where they are. But we are here for you. God bless ye. Wid you like tae say anythin', Sheila?

27

Sheila shakes her head. Thomas accepts her wish with a sincere nod of the head. There is a long silence.

Man, ah wish we'd goat some crisps. Ah'm starvin'.

EXT. FLAT. NIGHT

Michael rings the doorbell. Amanda opens the door.

MICHAEL

Alice in?

AMANDA

She's out.

MICHAEL

Right. You the baby-sitter?

AMANDA

Aye.

MICHAEL

Ah'm Michael. Ah'm the wanes' da.

AMANDA

Ah know. They've showed me photographs.

MICHAEL

They in their beds?

AMANDA

Aye.

MICHAEL

Dae ye mind if Ah use the toilet?

AMANDA

Naw. In ye come.

Michael goes in.

INT. TOILET. NIGHT

*Michael checks the bandage. It's more bloodied than he expected.
He buttons his shirt up again.*

INT. HALL. NIGHT

*Michael comes out of the toilet and there, standing in front of him,
is his son, David (aged six). David opens his arms sleepily. Michael
slowly crouches down and hugs him.*

> MICHAEL
> You're soakin'. You wet the bed?

> DAVID
> Naw.

> MICHAEL
> You jump intae bed wi' yer sister an' Ah'll change the sheets.

INT. KIDS' BEDROOM. NIGHT

*David is lying in bed with Angela (aged three). He watches as
Michael takes the sheets off the bed. Michael goes to overturn the
mattress but winces as the pain shoots through his stomach and he
puts the mattress down again. Amanda comes in, carrying the
sheets.*

> MICHAEL
> Could you give me a hand wi' this?

> AMANDA
> Sure.

*She puts down the sheets and they turn over the mattress. Michael
checks it.*

> MICHAEL
> It's damp as well.

AMANDA

He wet it last night. Alice told me. She said she wis gonny buy rubber sheets on Monday when she gets her money.

MICHAEL

David, son, ye're gonny have tae try an' go tae the toilet if ye need a pee. Otherwise yer bed's gonny be ruined.

David looks at his father innocently.

Right, well, ye're gonny have tae sleep wi' Angela the night, coz ye canny sleep in a damp bed.

DAVID

Can ah no sleep in Mummy's bed?

Michael looks to Angela, who shrugs, genuinely ignorant.

DAVID

Please, Dad. This bed's too wee.

MICHAEL

Aye, aw right. On ye go.

David leaps out of bed (he's now got a second wind).

DAVID

Will you read tae me?

MICHAEL

Sure.

INT. MUM'S BEDROOM. NIGHT

David jumps into his mother's bed and crawls under the sheets. Michael follows, looking decidedly uncomfortable, book in hand. He sits at the side of the bed.

MICHAEL
(*reading*)

'Once upon a time there was a little girl who lived in the

forest. Her name was Goldilocks. Now Goldilocks had always been told by her mother never . . .'

DAVID

Is Gran in heaven, Dad?

MICHAEL

Aye.

DAVID

An' is heaven far away, Dad?

MICHAEL

Aye.

DAVID

Further than the moon?

MICHAEL

A lot further.

DAVID

Can Ah visit her in heaven?

MICHAEL

Naw. Only dead people go tae heaven.

DAVID

Will she come an' visit me?

MICHAEL

Naw.

DAVID

Why not?

MICHAEL

Coz heaven's so nice an' friendly ye don't want tae come back.

DAVID

When Ah die will Ah go tae heaven, Dad?

MICHAEL

Course.

DAVID

When do ye die? When ye're old, like Gran?

MICHAEL

Right, nae mare questions, David. Ah thought you wanted to hear a story.

David has noticed something under the pillow. He pulls out a packet of condoms. Michael has continued reading.

DAVID

Dad, whit are they?

Michael looks down to see the condoms.

MICHAEL

Where did you find these?

DAVID

Under the pillow there.

MICHAEL
(*slamming the book shut*)
Right, put them back. Ye're sleeping in yer sister's bed.

DAVID

But Dad, you said Ah . . .

MICHAEL

David, do as ye're told please.

David throws the condoms down, gets out the bed and goes. Michael straightens up the bed, then picks up the condoms. He makes to put them under the pillow, then stops. He considers pocketing them for a minute, then puts them under the pillow. He leaves.

INT. CHINESE TAKE-AWAY. NIGHT

Tanga sits on the seats doing a crossword in the paper. A girl comes out of the kitchen and hands the carry-out over the counter with a slip. Tanga looks at the name and address.

> TANGA

Fuck! No' him.

The girl smiles. Tanga puts the carry-out into a blue container. John comes in.

> JOHN

Aw right, Tanga?

Tanga turns to see him.

> TANGA

Fuck, John, how ye doin'?

He goes across and gives John a huge bear hug.

Ah wis sorry tae hear aboot Aunt Rose. She wis a fine wummin. A very, very fine wummin.

> GIRL

Tanga.

> TANGA

Ah'm oan mah way.
> (to John)

Ye in fir a carry-oot?

> JOHN

Naw, Ah came in tae see you.

> TANGA

Well, this is mah last delivery the night. Ye fancy a wee jaunt an' then we'll go fir a few bevvies?

> JOHN

Aw right.

> **TANGA**
> (*driving*)

He stabbed Michael? Fuckin' hell. Never liked that sleazy cunt. Always goat the feelin' he'd like it up the arse but hasnae found a horse desperate enough.

> **JOHN**

Ah'm gonny kill him.

> **TANGA**

Fuckin' right. Stabbin' yer brother day before ye bury yer ma is a very killable offence.

> **JOHN**

Ah mean it.

> **TANGA**

Ah know ye dae.

> **JOHN**

Ye know where Ah could get mah hauns oan a gun?

> **TANGA**

Aye. But gettin' the gun's no, so much the problem as gettin' the ammo fir it.

> **JOHN**

How come?

> **TANGA**

Fuck knows. Aw Ah know is there's loads ah guys runnin' aboot here haudin' up shoaps wi' nae money wi' guns wi' nae fuckin' bullets. Sums this place up if ye ask me. How no' get somebody else tae dae it? You know big Harrison, don't ye? Fuck, man, he'll cut a guy's legs aff fur twenty Silk Cut and a rubber bone fir his dug.

> **JOHN**

Naw, Ah want tae dae it masel'.

Tanga nods to the blue container, which lies on the back seat.

> TANGA

Here, open that up fir us, wid ye? See if ye can find the beef wi' green peppers an' black bean sauce.

John stretches back and brings the container into the front seat. He opens it up and brings out one of the silver foil packages.

Ah hate this bastard. Always pays by cheque, never a tip, never a thank-you. Fuck all.
> (*he looks down*)

Nah, that's the beef an' mushroom. That's fir his missus. She's aw right. Thinks Ah'm hilarious, which, as you well know, Ah um. That's the one. Put it there, wid ye?

He opens the white cardboard lid with his free hand, snorts up a huge, disgusting gob and spits into the container.

> JOHN
> (*recoiling*)

Aw, fuck, man, that is disgustin'.

> TANGA

Of course it is. Black bean sauce – mingin'.

Tanga takes a screwdriver from the top of the dashboard and stirs it round. He then places the cardboard lid neatly back into position.

EXT. HOUSE. NIGHT

Tanga rings the doorbell. As he waits, he turns and pulls a face at John, who sits in the car. The door opens to reveal a large, sullen-faced man.

> TANGA

Evenin'.

MR BELL

How much?

TANGA

That's £12.75 please. That's includin' the delivery charge.

Mr Bell writes the cheque.

MR BELL

Has it gone up?

TANGA

'Fraid so, sir, 75p delivery charge now. Ridiculous, isn't it? Ah mean, that extra 25p could buy ye at least four or five prawn crackers. It's blatant profiteerin' if ye ask me.

Mrs Bell walks by behind him.

TANGA

Evenin', Mrs Bell.

She turns and smiles.

MRS BELL

Evenin'. Cold tonight.

TANGA

Freezin'.
(*to Mr Bell*)
Could ye put yer card number on the back please. Ta. An' it's very windy too. They're talkin' about gale force later on. An' it's a swine too, coz Ah wis thinkin' about takin' the yacht out tonight, y'know, me an' a few friends. We pooled wur tips last year an' that bought us a couple a bottles of fine wine an' the yacht came courtesy of twelve and a half million Embassy coupons . . .

Mr Bell grabs the carry-out, throws the cheque at Tanga and slams the door shut.

INT. CAR. NIGHT

Tanga jumps into the car.

> **TANGA**
>
> Bastard cut me right in the middle of mah fuckin' gag! Ah hate that? Why dae people dae that?

> **JOHN**
>
> Dunno.

> **TANGA**
>
> Coz they're jealous. They might have the big hoose, the fancy car an' the beautiful wife, but whit they really want is tae be me. Ahm Ah right?

> **JOHN**
>
> Sure, Tanga.

> **TANGA**
>
> Don't talk pish. Why the fuck wid he want tae be me? Thirty-five year old an' deliverin' Chinkies. Ah don't fuckin' think so, ya patronizin' wee cunt.

> **JOHN**
>
> Dae ye know where Ah can get a gun?

> **TANGA**
>
> Ye're no listenin' tae me, John. Ah'm a very sensitive man an' that cunt hurt mah feelings. Ah'll no have anybody look doon at me. Nobody. You understand whit Ah'm sayin'?

> **JOHN**
> (*trying to diffuse the situation*)
>
> Aye.

> **TANGA**
>
> Good. Right, let's go an' see about gettin' ye a gun. Ye like Connolly? Course ye dae. Everybody loves Connolly.

He puts on a tape of Billy Connolly Live. *They drive off.*

INT. KIDS' BEDROOM. NIGHT

Michael sits in the darkness wrapped up in his own thoughts. The kids are fast asleep. He hears the front door open and suddenly jumps up. He hears Amanda talking to his wife. In a panic he hides behind the door. The door opens.

                    AMANDA
        Ah thought he was in here. He must have left.

Alice looks into the bedroom and can see Michael, his head turned to the wall, in the cupboard mirror.

                    ALICE
        Yer taxi's down the stairs, Amanda.

She gives her £10.

        Thanks a lot.

They step into the hall, leaving the door open. We hear Amanda going out and Alice walks back into the sitting room. Michael waits a few moments, then makes his exit. Just as he gets to the front door, we hear:

        How are they all doin'?

Michael stops. Alice steps out of the living room.

                    MICHAEL
        They're aw right.
                    (*pause*)
        We're a family, y' know. Things like this brings ye thegither.

                    ALICE
        Ah'm sure.

Pause.

                    MICHAEL
        Where wur ye the night?

ALICE

Mah AA meetin'!

MICHAEL

Right.
(*he laughs awkwardly*)
Christ, the idea of bein' stone-cold sober That wid really dae mah head in.

ALICE

Whit time's the funeral tomorrow.

MICHAEL

Ten. Ye comin'?

ALICE

Of course.

MICHAEL

Listen, Ah'm due a bonus at work so Ah thought Ah'd buy tha wanes bunk beds. That'd be aw right, widn't it?.

ALICE

Aye.

MICHAEL

Right, well Ah'm away tae get pissed. Ah'll see ye.

ALICE

See ye.

Alice walks back into the sitting room, turning the light off as she does so. Significantly, however, she leaves the door open. From the hallway Michael can see the warm glow of the fire and the flickering light of the television. For a moment he considers joining her. But the moment passes and he leaves.

EXT. SMALL CARNIVAL ON A PIECE OF WASTEGROUND. NIGHT

John stands outside one of the caravans. Tanga opens the door.

TANGA

Here, stick that under yer juke.

He gives John a long object in a white polythene bag. John immediately puts it under his jacket.

JOHN
(*excitedly*)

Is that it?

TANGA

Aye. How?

JOHN

Nothin'. Fuckin' big, in't it?

TANGA

So?

JOHN

Nothin'. How much?

TANGA

Give us a couple of minutes. Ah might be able tae get it for nothin'.

Tanga goes back inside. John looks about, then goes round the side of the caravan. He opens his jacket and looks inside the bag. He slowly brings out a thick, steely, sawn-off shotgun. He is totally entranced by it. Snapping out of it, he puts the bag in his pocket and secretes the gun under his jacket. He walks round to the front of the caravan grinning like a naughty child. As she looks round, he sees Rab with his friends jumping on to the Spider (the fairground ride where each carriage interweaves, the speed building up and taking them to and from the perimeter). John walks over to it and stands at the edge. The lads' carriage spins outward and they see John staring at them. As they pull away they laugh at him and give him the finger, etc. John slips his hand inside his jacket. He looks round to make sure nobody's looking. As their carriage comes back to the perimeter John swiftly takes out the

gun, just long enough for them to see it and be suitably terrified.
John hides the gun again, waiting joyfully for his prey to return.
Their carriage whizzes out again and, with a quick look round,
John brings the gun full out, leans over the perimeter and aims it
straight at the faces of those poor kids. They make a pathetic
attempt to cover themselves before they spin away again. As the
music blares with the joyful screaming of the other passengers, we
stay on Rab and his friends, who desperately try and find a way off
their carriage, but the safety bar is bolted tight. As they return to
the spot they huddle together in terrified expectation. When they
glimpse up, however, they see that John has gone.

INT. CAR DRIVING ALONG THE ROAD. NIGHT

John is yelping with excitement.

> JOHN
> Ah'm tellin' ye, Tanga, it felt so fuckin' good! Ah never
> thought Ah'd feel good again.

> TANGA
> Whit, terrifyin' wee boys?

> JOHN
> Aw, fuck, Ah wis only pissin' aboot. Ah just wanted tae teach
> them a lesson. Ah widnae have done it if it wis loaded.

> TANGA
> An' whit ye gonny dae when it is loaded?

> JOHN
> Whit dae ye thin Ah'm gonny dae?

> TANGA
> Tell me.

> JOHN
> Ah'm gonny shoot Duncan.

TANGA

Ye better.

JOHN

Ah will. Don't you worry.

TANGA

Ah'm no. But don't let me down.
(*pause*)
Right, then it's mah turn.

JOHN

Whit ye talkin' aboot?

TANGA

Ah want a wee shot of it. Why should you get aw the fun?

John doesn't know what to say, but Tanga just smiles and puts the Connolly *tape back on.*

INT. CHAPEL. NIGHT

Thomas lights a candle and smiles up to the beneficent face of the Virgin Mary. Sheila is parked nearby.

SHEILA

Thomas,   ah   want   to   go   home.

THOMAS

(*knowing how difficult it is for her to speak*)
What?

SHEILA

(*with even greater effort*)
I   want   to   go   home.

THOMAS

We can't, Sheila. Ah promised Father Fitzgerald and Ah promised Mum we'd stay the night.

SHEILA

You did. I didn't.

THOMAS

Sheila, Ah can't leave here an' you can't go home yourself, so you'll just have to stay. Are you cold?

SHEILA

No.

THOMAS

You can have mah jacket.

SHEILA

I want to go home.

THOMAS

Even if Ah let you go by yourself, how would you get in the house?

SHEILA

Michael or John could let me in.

THOMAS

But how do ye know they're there? They're probably out clubbin' it. No. I'm sorry, Sheila, Ah can't allow that.

He turns to look up again at the Virgin Mary. An enraged Sheila slams her hand down on the 'go' button and she hurls towards Thomas, ramming right into the back of him. He goes crashing into the candle stance, which in turn pushes against the stand and so the Virgin Mary falls to the floor and breaks into pieces. Thomas stares in disbelief.

My God, Sheila, whit have you done? Ye've smashed the Virgin Mary. Ah don't know whit kind of sin that is but, bloody hell, Sheila, it'll be a big one.

SHEILA

You let me out of here.

THOMAS

You want out? Right, fair enough. You can go!

Thomas charges up the aisle, followed quickly by Sheila. He mutters constantly as he walks to the door and opens it.

Ah'll have tae fix it. Father Fitzgerald will go bloody ape-shit. Christ almighty! An' Ah'm gonny have tae pray fir you, Sheila. Ah'm gonny have tae say a lotta prayers fir you.

The door opens and Sheila leaves, going down the ramp at the side. Thomas shouts after her:

An' when ye see the other two, tell them it was your idea, no mine, an' remember, it's ten o'clock tomorrow. You lot better not be late! Ah can't do all this by myself, you know.

Thomas goes back inside. He marches angrily into the chapel and down the aisle, slowly coming to a halt by his mother's coffin. For a moment he's almost frightened, as if his mother might jump out and chastise him for what he's done. But as he takes in the situation – the coffin, the altar, the plush red carpet around it, the dark beauty of the chapel – he realizes that he is alone. Alone at last with his sad, unseen, unheard mother. He steps forward and pats the coffin.

Sheila's had to go, Mum. She was gettin' cold. Ah know you were never keen on her goin' out by herself at night, but there was no stoppin' her. She's grown up a lot in the last few days. We all have. You understand, Ah know ye do. But Ah'm still here fir ye, Ma. Ah'm no gaun any place. That's a promise.

He looks across at the smashed Madonna and lets out a heavy 'work to be done' sigh. He takes off his jacket, lays it over one of the benches and begins the arduous task of reassembling the broken statue.

EXT. STREET. NIGHT

Through the dimly lit street Sheila is driving along, muttering angrily to herself. Suddenly she looks up to see a small set of headlights coming straight towards her. She swerves and only narrowly avoids crashing into what is revealed as a small motorized car driven by an even smaller boy. His mother runs up, stopping by Sheila and shouting after her son:

MOTHER
(who speaks with a relatively posh accent)
Edward! Would you bloody well slow down!
(to Sheila)
You all right? He's like his father, drives like a maniac. Are you sure you're all right? Is there someone with you?

Sheila starts up and almost runs the woman over as she goes.

Well, fuck you.
(she suddenly remembers Edward)
Edward! Watch the man's dog.

We hear a yelp and a man cursing as we watch Sheila disappear around the corner.

EXT. MR BELL'S HOUSE. NIGHT

Tanga and John creep round the back of the house. They stop underneath a window about six feet off the ground. They see it's open about twelve inches. Tanga gets a bunky-up from John and looks through the window. Inside we see it's a bathroom. Just by the window he can see Mr Bell stood over the sink, his trousers down. He is masturbating over a porn magazine, which lies opened on the cistern. Tanga nearly chokes holding back his guffaw. He signals John to let him down. He tries to explain what he's seen in a whisper while trying to contain his hysteria.

TANGA
He's . . . he's . . . he's havin' a wank.

JOHN

Whit?

TANGA

He's up there pullin' his plug.

They both have to cover their mouths to stop themselves laughing out loud.

Right, gie us it.

John gives him the gun, then gives him a bunky-up. Tanga carefully puts the gun through the window till it's only a few inches from Mr Bell's backside. Tanga waits for his moment.

Ah'll show ye mine if you show me yours.

Mr Bell turns in panic. A second, then the poor man ejaculates over a smirking Tanga's face.

From below John hears Tanga scream before he comes crashing down to the ground, frantically clawing at his face as if he'd been burnt by acid. John tries to calm him down.

JOHN

Whit's the matter? Whit's the matter?

TANGA
(*almost screaming*)

He came in mah face! The bastard came aw oer mah fuckin' face!

There is a brief frozen pause before Tanga starts again.

Aw, fuck! Aw, fuck! Ah can taste it. Ah can fuckin' taste it. Ah'm gonny be sick.

He gags, then suddenly starts walking to the front of the house.

Ah'm gonny get that bastard. Ah'm gonny smash his fuckin' jaw in.

JOHN

Tanga. Tanga. Yer forgettin', we don't huv any bullets.

TANGA

This is aw we need.

They come round to the front of the house. Tanga kicks the door in.

INT. HOUSE. NIGHT

Tanga and John run through the hall. A quick look and they see the bathroom is empty. They run into the sitting room, where a shocked Mrs Bell is watching TV. Mr Bell, who's been on the phone, drops it and runs into the kitchen, where he picks up a large kitchen knife. Tanga has followed him in.

TANGA
(in a panicked rage)

Drop the knife! Drop the fuckin' knife or Ah'll fuckin' blast yer head off!

Mr Bell holds on to the knife.

Fuckin' drop it!!

Mr Bell still holds on to the knife, more through terror than anything else. Tanga speaks to John:

Keep an eye on her.
(to Mr Bell)

You! Ah'm gonny tell you wan mare time, then Ah'm gonny shoot ye. Ye understaun? Noo drop the fuckin' knife!

Mr Bell still holds on to the knife.

Whit is it wi' you? Ye want tae fuckin' die? John, bring her in here.

John brings in Mrs Bell.

Tell this wanker husband ah yours tae drop that fuckin' knife.

47

Mrs Bell is in a state of shock and can manage only to open her mouth, but no words come out.

Whit the fuck is it wi' you two? You want me tae fuckin' shoot him? Coz Ah'll dae it if ye want me tae. Ye want me tae?

Mrs Bell shakes her head.

Ah think ye do. Ah think you want me. Ah knew it, man. Knew you fuckin' fancied me. John, haud this.

He hands John the gun.

If that fuckin' prick moves fae there, you blast him.

He winks at John.

JOHN

Where you gaun?

TANGA

Ah'm gaun upstairs wi' Mrs Bell.

Mr Bell moves forward but stops as John points the gun at him.

JOHN

Whit ye talkin' aboot?

TANGA

Ah'm oan mah hole. She's always been intae me. C'mon, darlin'!

He puts his arm around Mrs Bell and starts moving her towards the sitting-room door. She resists, but Tanga has a strong grip.

JOHN

Get yer fuckin' hauns aff her.

TANGA

Whit?

JOHN

Just leave her. An we'll get out of here, aw right?

TANGA

Fuck off. Mah baws are like melons, man. She's intae it, Ah'm tellin' ye.

JOHN
(*pointing the gun at him*)
Ah'll fuckin' shoot ye.

A moment, then Tanga laughs long and hard.

TANGA

You really huv lost it the night, man. You forgettin' that ye huvnae any fuckin' . . .

Tanga just manages to stop himself.

JOHN

Havnae any whit?
(*to Mr Bell*)
You get out here.

John, pointing the gun between Tanga and Mr Bell, walks backwards into the sitting room and stops Mr Bell at a point where he's within striking distance of Tanga.

Havnae any whit, Tanga? Havnae any bottle? Is that whit ye wur gonny say?

Tanga looks at Mr Bell, who is gearing himself to pounce.

Is that whit ye were gonny say? That Ah havnae any bottle? Maybe ye're right. Maybe Ah should just drop this gun and let this cunt at ye.

TANGA
(*to Mr Bell*)
Don't you even think about it. He's just windin' me up, man. You come near me, he'll kill you.

JOHN

Ah will inaw. An' Ah'll kill you if you're no' oot that door in five seconds.

50

Tanga weighs up the situation.

> TANGA

Fuck the lotta yez.

> (*to Mrs Bell*)

Yer man's a fuckin' wanker.

He goes. John slowly backs out behind him, keeping the gun pointed at Mr Bell.

INT. TANGA'S CAR. NIGHT

They are driving along the road.

> JOHN

First chance Ah get Ah'm gonny boot fuck oot you, ya sick fuck.

> TANGA

Any time, ya prick. Any time.

> JOHN

Ah fuckin' mean it.

> TANGA

Ye want tae come ahead? Eh? Ye want tae come ahead?

Tanga slaps him across the face with the back of his left hand. John makes to retaliate, but Tanga swerves the car wildly. John thinks the better of it. Tanga slaps him again.

C'mon, ya shitebag. Come ahead.

> JOHN

Stop the motor. Stop the motor an' Ah'll fuckin' . . .

Tanga hits him again.

> TANGA
> (*screaming*)

Come on, ya bastard!!!

Tanga takes his right hand off the wheel and cracks John with a full punch on the face. Seeing its effect, he pulls into the side of the road and starts punching into John. John responds with two vicious blows to Tanga's head. As Tanga tries to protect himself, John follows through, punching him repeatedly on the head. Tanga surrenders.

Aw right, aw right.

John punches him one more time then backs off. Tanga is still covering himself.

Ya fuckin' shitebag.

John punches into him once again.

JOHN
Who's a shitebag? Who's a shitebag?

Tanga comes out from under his guard.

TANGA
You ur! No way are you gonny see this through.

JOHN
You get me the bullets an' you watch me shoot that cunt. Ah'll dae it. Believe me, Ah'll dae it.

TANGA
Swear oan yer ma's grave!

JOHN
Whit?

TANGA
Swear oan yer ma's grave!

JOHN
A'm no' a fuckin' wane.

TANGA
Then it shouldnae bother ye. Swear oan yer ma's grave ye're

gonny kill Duncan. Or ye can forget about the bullets.

JOHN

Mah ma's goat fuck all tae dae wi' this.

TANGA

Good. Ah'm pleased fir ye. Now dae it.

John thinks long and hard before answering.

JOHN

Ah swear on mah ma's grave that Ah will kill Duncan.

TANGA
(*with mock horror*)
That is a terrible thing that you've just said. Y'know that?
Your ma would never have hurt nobody and here you are
swearin' oan her grave, a grave that she's no' even been laid
tae rest in, that you're gonny kill a guy.

Tanga starts up the car.

Ah, well, you're one wane she'll no' be meetin' in heaven.
Hell's fire here we come.

*He grins demonically at John, who can barely conceal his fear at
the vow he has just made. They drive off.*

EXT. STREET. NIGHT

*Sheila drives along the street. She comes to an alleyway and turns
into it. Midway down her wheelchair stops. She hits the 'go' button
and jerks forward a few inches, then nothing. She is stranded. She
hears some people walking along the street behind her. She tries to
turn her head and shout for assistance but can't. Slowly she becomes
more and more apprehensive as the reality of her plight begins to
sink in. It's cold, it's dark and she can't move by herself. Then she
hears a mouth organ. It's distant but getting closer. Out of the
darkness, striding along merrily, comes Carole (aged ten), who is
playing said mouth organ. In her left hand she has a polythene bag,*

inside of which is a birthday cake. On her head she has a pointed, pink 'princess hat', which has a long, tacky veil running down the back. A scabby dog runs ahead of her and stands barking at Sheila.

CAROLE
(*taking the mouth organ from her mouth*)
Kimberley! Stop that.

Kimberley keeps barking.

Kimberley! Ah said stop that!

Kimberley slowly skulks away. Carole speaks to Sheila.

Whit's the matter? You stuck?

Sheila nods.

You want a push?

SHEILA
Please.

CAROLE
Where ye gaun?

SHEILA
Home.

CAROLE
You want tae come tae a birthday party? It's a surprise for mah da. Ye want tae come? 'Mon, Ah'll gie a push.

Carole goes behind Sheila and tries to push the wheelchair, but it's very heavy.

Man, this thing weighs a ton. You wait there an' Ah'll get somebody tae gie us a haun. Kimberley! You stay here. Stay!

Before Sheila can say anything Carole is off, merrily blasting on her mouth organ. Kimberley sits forlorn (much like Sheila) and after a few moments begins to whine after his mistress. Sheila makes a brave attempt to communicate with this sad mutt.

54

It's all right. She'll be back in a minute.

Kimberley immediately takes this momentary kindness to mean lasting affection and before Sheila has even finished speaking she's up on Sheila's lap and licking her face. Sheila twists her face away but to no effect. We hear Carole:

CAROLE

Kimberley! You get aff ah there!

Carole runs down the alley, followed by three paper-girls, Ann-Marie, Melissa and Bernadette. Each girl has a satchel full of the night edition of the Daily Record. *The girls circle round Sheila and fire questions at her, not waiting for an answer.*

ANN-MARIE

Ye lost?

MELISSA

Ye want us tae gie ye a haun?

BERNADETTE
(*to Carole*)

Can she talk?

CAROLE

Aye.

ANN-MARIE

You said she wis a spastic.

MELISSA

Fuck sake, Ann-Marie, watch whit ye're sayin'.

ANN-MARIE

Wisnae me that said it. It wis her. Fuck.

MELISSA

We're gonny gie ye a shove doon tae Carole's hoose, aw right?

                    BERNADETTE
                    (*to Carole*)
Can she read?

                    (*to Sheila*)
Ye want tae buy a *Record*?

                    MELISSA
Right, let's gie her a shove.

They go behind the wheelchair and start pushing.

EXT. STREET. NIGHT

*Carole leads the way, playing her mouth organ. Behind her is
Sheila, being pushed by the girls. And behind them is Kimberley.*

                    MELISSA
Carole!

Carole stops.

Can ye no' play a tune oan that thing?

*Carole thinks for a second, then begins the only real tune she
knows: 'Some Day My Prince Will Come'.*

                    ANNE-MARIE
Whit the fuck's that?

                    CAROLE
                    (*stopping playing for a second*)
Snow White.

*She carries on playing. Melissa is the first to join in, followed
playfully by the other two. Sheila is simply bewildered by the
whole affair.*

EXT. STREET. NIGHT

The girls stand at the top of a slight hill.

MELISSA
Right, be careful. Nae runnin'.

They set off slowly at first, but the weight of the wheelchair soon takes over and the girls find themselves barely able to hold on to it as it moves faster and faster towards the bottom. Ann-Marie loses her footing and trips, her papers scattering everywhere. The other girls don't stop until they have safely got Sheila to the bottom. They look back at Ann-Marie, who is spread-eagled on the pavement and in the excitement they laugh

ANN-MARIE
(*almost in tears*)
It's no' fuckin' funny!

Melissa and Bernadette stop laughing and walk back up to her, picking papers up on the way.

Aw, Jesus, man. Look at mah papers. Fuckin' wrecked.

BERNADETTE
(*sympathetically*)
Fuck, Ann-Marie, whit ye gonny dae?

ANN-MARIE
Dunno. Aw, fuck, that's me man. Billy's gonny sack me fir that.

MELISSA
Naw, he willnae.

ANN-MARIE
Aye, he fuckin' will!

MELISSA
Just get him tae dock it aff yer money.

ANN-MARIE
He'll dae that anyway. Then he'll fuckin' sack me.>

Carole blasts on her mouth organ.

58

CAROLE

We'll need tae go. Ah'm gonny be late.

ANN-MARIE
(*exploding*)
Fuckin' shut it, you! This is aw your fault, ya stupit wee cow.

CAROLE

How's it mah fault?

ANN-MARIE

Fuckin' getting' us tae push some spaz up the road! It widnae huv happened if it wisnae fir you!

MELISSA
(*to Ann-Marie*)
How many ye lost?

Ann-Marie does a very rough count.

ANN-MARIE

About thirty.

MELISSA

Right, fours £1. So that's whit? Seven fours are twenty-eight. It's about £7.50. Fuck. Ah can gie ye about three quid.

Bernadette goes into her pockets.

BERNADETTE

Sorry, Ann-Marie, Ah've only got about £1.

She brings out her change and they gather round counting. Carole approaches them.

CAROLE

Here!

Carole holds out a £10 note.

ANNE-MARIE

Where did you get that?

59

Carole points to Sheila.

CAROLE

She gave me it.

Ann-Marie, Melissa and Bernadette walk over curiously to Sheila.

MELISSA

You know that's £10?

Sheila nods.

And you want tae gie it tae Ann-Marie?

Sheila nods again. They look at her like she's insane.

ANN-MARIE

If ye tell me where ye live, Ah'll make sure ye get it back.

Sheila shakes her head.

ANN-MARIE

Ah will. That's a promise.

CAROLE

Can we go now?

ANN-MARIE

Well, Ah canny push coz mah hauns are aw skint.

MELISSA
(half laughing)

Fuckin' hell, Ann-Marie. You ur wan moaney cow.

ANN-MARIE

Well, they ur!

BERNADETTE

Maybe we should put you in the wheelchair.

ANN-MARIE

Fuck, man, ah wis just sayin'.

They start to push, moaning and joking as they go. Carole starts

60

*playing the mouth organ again. Sheila seems more relaxed. In fact,
she almost seems to be enjoying herself now.*

INT./EXT. CAROLE'S TENEMENT FLAT. NIGHT

*Louise (aged seven) is playing with her wee brother, Luke (aged
four). She hears Carole's mouth organ and runs to the window.
She sees Carole and the others.*

> LOUISE

Mum! It's Carole!

Louise opens the window.

Carole! You're dead!

> CAROLE
> (*shouting*)

Shut it, you!

Alison (Carole's mum) comes to the window.

> ALISON

Carole, where the hell you been? Get in here now!

> CAROLE

Ma, Ah wis . . .

> ALISON

In here, now!

*Carole starts to walk up the ramp that runs down the front of the
flats. An elderly woman, Mrs Finch, raps on her window before
opening it.*

> MRS FINCH

Ah've told you before no tae walk up there. That ramp's for
me. That's who it was built for. Noo, go up the stairs.

Carole mutters under her breath and walks back down.

MELISSA

Carole, where you goin'?

CAROLE

Ah've got tae go in.

MELISSA
(*looking to Sheila*)
Whit aboot her?

CAROLE

Ah've goat tae go in.

Carole goes up the stairs and into the close, leaving the girls severely gobsmacked.

BERNADETTE
(*to Melissa*)
We're gonny have tae go or we're gonny miss the pubs comin' out.

ANN-MARIE

C'mon, we better go.

MELISSA

We canny just leave her here.

ANN-MARIE

We'll come back.
(*to Sheila*)
We need tae go an' sell our papers but we'll come back fir ye, OK?

Sheila stares at her blankly.

MELISSA

We'll come back, promise.

The girls, more than a little embarrassed, go.

INT. CAROLE'S HOUSE. NIGHT

Alison has been watching this. Carole stands repentant beside her.

> ALISON
>
> Where the hell are they gaun? Whit they daen leavin' that lassie there?

> CAROLE
>
> She's wi' me.

> ALISON
>
> Whit?

> CAROLE
>
> Her wheelchair broke an' Ah said she could come tae Da's party.

> ALISON
>
> For Christ sake, Carole, whit is it wi' you? Maist wanes bring home stray cats but no' you. You've goat tae bring home a . . . Right. Stay here.

EXT. STREET OUTSIDE CAROLE'S FLAT. NIGHT

Sheila sits stunned by all this. She looks around this strange and unfamiliar street. She tries the 'go' button again but to no effect. She looks to the window where Mrs Finch sits. She looks to the other window, where Carole, Louise and wee Luke stand. Carole waves pathetically as Alison comes out. Alison walks briskly to Sheila.

> ALISON
>
> What's your name?
>
> *(no reply)*
>
> Where dae ye stay?
>
> *(no reply)*
>
> Can ye speak?

SHEILA
(*utterly pissed off*)

F- f– fuck off!

ALISON
(*apologetically*)

Ah'm sorry. Ah didnae know ye wir wi' Carole. Ah thought ye wir wi' them. Ye want tae come in?

Sheila does not reply.

C'mon.

She goes behind the wheelchair and starts pushing Sheila up the ramp. Mrs Finch raps the window.

MRS FINCH

That's mah ramp.

ALISON

Aw, fir Christ sake, Alice, ah canny get her up the stair masel'.

MRS FINCH

That ramp wis built fir me.

ALISON

Ye want me just tae leave the lassie? Her chair's broke.

MRS FINCH

Ah don't care. Ah'm fed up wi' people thinkin' that's a short cut. It's mah ramp. Mah husband, God rest his soul, fought for three years tae get that built.

ALISON

Alice, Ah'm no gonny stand here arguin' wi' ye. Ah need tae get the lassie inside before she gets pneumonia.

MRS FINCH

Ye're no' usin' it an' that's final.

CAROLE
(*shouting from window*)
Why don't you shut it, ya old bag!

ALISON
Carole! Don't you dare speak to Mrs Finch like that.

MRS FINCH
That lassie should be in a home.

ALISON
Aw, Alice, fuck up an' gie us peace.

She starts pushing Sheila up the ramp.

MRS FINCH
That's it! Ah'm phonin' the polis! Get aff mah ramp. That's mah ramp.

Alison ignores all this and they go inside.

INT. CAROLE'S HOUSE. NIGHT

Alison comes into the hallway pushing Sheila. The kids walk backwards, fascinated by this new visitor. Louise has a bunch of balloons in her hand.

ALISON
Right out the way. Ah said out the way.

Alison direct Sheila into the kitchen.

CAROLE
You said the 'f' word to Mrs Finch. Ah heard ye. Ye said the 'f' word!

ALISON
Don't give me any lip, mah girl. You're in enough trouble as it is. Where the hell have you been? Ye shouldn't have been more than ten minutes and you've been nearly an hour! Ah wis worried sick!

CAROLE

Afzals only had one chocolate cake an' you told me no' tae get chocolate, so Ah went tae Imrans.

ALISON

Imrans is bloody miles away. Anthin' could have happened tae ye.

CAROLE

Ah had Kimberley!

ALISON

Kimberley widnae have been any use tae ye if the polis had picked ye up, wid she? Well, would she?

Kimberley starts to bark as the shouting level increases.

Kimberley, shut it!

Louise stands in front of Sheila with her balloons, smiling. By this time Alison towers over Carole as their furious argument ensues. Kimberley continues barking.

Kimberley. Out! Out!

CAROLE

Don't take it out oan Kimberley!

ALISON

Don't you raise yer voice at me. Kimberley is a dog. You are a wee lassie. An' the two of you will do as you're told. Do you understand me?

LOUISE.

Mum!

ALISON
(*without looking round*)

Quiet, Louise.
(*to Carole*)

Now what the hell dae you think you're doin' pushin' people

around in wheelchairs at eleven o'clock at night? Where did ye find her, for Christ's sake?

CAROLE

She wis stuck! Ah wis tryin' to help her.

LOUISE

Mum!

ALISON

Helpin' her is one thing, bringin' her home is another!

LOUISE

Mum!

ALISON

What is it, Louise?

Alison turns around to see the wheelchair is empty. Looking to the ground, she sees Sheila lying on the floor screaming silently. Alison, understandably, mistakes this as some kind of epileptic fit.

Carole, phone 999 and ask for an ambulance.

SHEILA

No! Ah don't want an ambulance. Ah don't want anythin'! Just leave me. Ah can doo things for myself! Ah'm no bloody stupid! Mah batteries went flat. That was all. Mah batteries went flat. That's aw there is tae it. Mah batteries went flat Bloody batteries!

She makes an attempt to kick the wheelchair but she's clearly exhausted. Alison can only look on, waiting for her to calm down.

INT. CAROLE'S HOUSE. NIGHT

The living room has been decorated for a surprise party for Ed, the kids' dad and Alison's husband. The kids sit on the sofa staring intently at Sheila. Carole holds a cup of tea, from which Sheila drinks. Alison sits on the chair nearby.

SHEILA

Ah'm   sorry   Ah   lost   mah   temper.

ALISON

Naw, Ah'm sorry, Ah lost mine as well. Ah just didnae know what was goin' on.

SHEILA

Me   neither.

Sheila laughs. Alison responds in kind, now beginning to feel more comfortable knowing that Sheila is neither mentally handicapped nor dangerous.

ALISON

There must be somebody lookin' fir ye. Yer mum an' dad?

SHEILA

They're dead.

ALISON

Any other family?

SHEILA

Three brothers.

ALISON

Where are they?

Sheila considers telling her the whole saga but decides otherwise. Alison notices.

Are they at home?

SHEILA

They might be.

ALISON

Why don't we give them a call and maybe they can come an' pick ye up.

CAROLE

No way. She's stayin' fir the party, in't ye?

ALISON

Well, let's give them a call and let them know she's all right.
Louise, hand the phone over, wid ye?

Louise picks up the cordless phone.

LOUISE

Can Ah dial the numbers please, Mum?

Alison sighs but decides to keep the peace.

ALISON
(*to Sheila*)

What's your number?

Sheila says the umber, which Louise dutifully punches into the phone.

LOUISE

It's ringing.

*She holds the phone up and we hear the faint ringing sounds.
Sheila knows no one will answer. Alison senses also that things are
not what they should be. As she feels Sheila's mood begin to drop,
she jumps up.*

ALISON

Right then. Let's get these balloons up. Yer father will be home
soon.
(*to Sheila*)
So you'll be stayin' for the party then?

*Sheila makes no reply. Alison takes the phone from Louise and
puts it back down on the receiver.*

INT. HANGMAN'S BAR. NIGHT

*The young barman hands Michael a pint. Michael hands over the
money. Hanson, the owner of the pub, screams in his ear.*

HANSON

Finish up yer drinks now please!

MICHAEL
(*quietly*)

Christ, Ah've just goat it.

HANSON
(*turning on him*)

Whit?

MICHAEL

Ah said Ah've just got it.

HANSON

Well, hurry up an' finish it then. That's time!

Hanson moves through the bar, shouting and picking up glasses.

Finish yer drinks now please!

A woman appears beside Michael with a collecting can.

WOMAN

Would you like to give to the Sick Children's Hospital?

Michael goes into his pocket, but just as he's about to put money into the can Hanson moves in.

HANSON
(*to woman*)

Right, you, get the fuck out of here. Ah've told you before, ye've goat tae have a licence.

WOMAN
(*showing her badge*)

I've got a licence.

HANSON

Ah don't care. Get tae fuck. Now!

The woman goes. Hanson slams down a pile of stinking ashtrays beside Michael.

MICHAEL

You goat somethin' against sick kids?

HANSON
(*smiling*)

Aye, Ah fuckin' hate them. Wish they'd aw hurry up an' die. Now finish yer drinks now please!

Melissa comes into the bar.

MELISSA

Daily Record!

HANSON

Gie us two.

She hands him two newspapers. He gives her the money.

Right, now out of here.

Melissa draws him a deadly look but does as she's told. Hanson puts the papers on the bar beside the ashtrays and Michael. Michael sips his pint and twists his head round to read the headlines. Hanson pulls the papers away.

Get yer ane! An' finish yer drink. Ah'll no' tell ye again!

MICHAEL
(*his patience exhausted*)

Whit the fuck is your problem?

HANSON

You gonny gie me trouble? You gonny gie me trouble?

He suddenly grabs Michael by the neck and pushes him towards the end of the bar.

Alistair! Open the door.

Alistair, the barman, runs to the end of the bar and unbolts a thick, wooden door. Hanson pushes the stunned Michael in. He then turns to the few remaining customers.

Now finish yer drinks! That's time!

INT. CELLAR. NIGHT

Michael kicks the door.

> MICHAEL
> Open this door, ya fuckin' maniac!

> HENRY
> (*voice-over*)
> Ah widnae kick the door, son. That'll make him really angry.

Michael turns and sees Henry and his wife, Minnie, stood against the back wall.

> MICHAEL
> Whit the fuck's goin' on here?

> HENRY
> He's in a foul mood tonight.
> (*to Minnie*)
> Ah telt ye we should've gone tae the Anchor.

> MINNIE
> (*sarcastically*)
> Aye, so ye did. Goat a fag on ye, son?

Michael brings out a pack of cigarettes.

> HENRY
> Ah widnae mind won inaw if ye can afford it, son.

Michael gives them each a cigarette. Henry speaks to Minnie:

> Think he'll mind us smokin'?

> MINNIE
> Fuck him. We canny smoke in the jail.

HENRY
(to Michael)
Think he'll mind us smokin'?

MICHAEL
Dunno. Whit dae ye mean 'in the jail'?

MINNIE
After he's locked up he'll phone the polis, then they'll come
doon an' that'll be us fir the weekend.
(to Henry)
An it's aw your fault!

HENRY
It's no mah fault.
(to Michael)
She wis tryin' tae strangle me. Look at that. See the marks oan
mah neck?

He shows Michael his neck.

MINNIE
Ah well, ye deserved it. Chattin' up that fat slag.

HENRY
Ah wisnae chattin' her up. We wur talkin' aboot Jean de
Florette an' Manon des Sources.
(to Michael)
She speaks fluent French.

MINNIE
Aye, an' you talk constant pish.

MICHAEL
Ah canny afford tae go tae jail. This is fuckin' madness. The
cunt canny lock us in here like it's a fuckin' holdin' cell.

HENRY
Polis love him, son. They love him.

MINNIE

Whit ye in fir?

MICHAEL

Ah looked at his *Daily Record.*

MINNIE

That's terrible. He's really lost it the night.

Seamus emerges from behind an empty beer keg.

SEAMUS

That's nothin', man. Ah put mah feet oan a chair. Oan a fuckin' chair. Cunt puts me in here fir that. Can ye believe it? He wis like that 'Get yer feet aff the chair' an Ah wis like that 'Aw right, calm doon, man. Nae offence. Just wanted tae make masel' more comfortable.' Fuck ye. Cunts like that. In there man. Ah've been in here since seven o'clock. Missed the quiz night an' everythin'.

MICHAEL

Anybody else in here? Like a flute band or women's aerobic class.

SEAMUS

Naw, just us.

MICHAEL

Any other way oot ah here?

HENRY

'Fraid not, son.

Michael looks around and sees an unopened beer keg.

MICHALE
(*to Seamus*)

Here, gie us a haun wi' that.

INT. PUB. NIGHT

Alistair is washing glasses. Hanson is counting the till money.
Alistair looks at door and sees smoke coming out the bottom.

> ALISTAIR

Mr Hanson!

Hanson looks to him, then to the door.

> HANSON

What the fuck!

Hanson goes over to the door and starts banging on it.

You lot better no' have damaged mah property! Ye hear me?
Ah'll make sure ye get three year if ye huv!

INT. CELLAR. NIGHT

Michael and Seamus stand holding the beer keg at either end.
Minnie and Henry are blowing smoke through the bottom of the
door. They hear the sound of the bolt being pulled back. Michael
nods and with a yell he and Seamus throw the beer keg though the
door, taking it off its hinges and smashing down on Hanson.
Minnie howls with glee and proceeds to jump on the door,
flattening an already flattened Hanson. Alistair looks on, helpless.
Michael holds his side in obvious pain.

INT. PUB TOILET. NIGHT

In the cubicle we pan up to see a pair of trousers on the floor and a
pair of legs wrapped in plastic bags, Sellotaped like leggings. As we
move up, we see it's Michael putting the finishing touches to his
torso, which is similarly wrapped. His hands are bloody.

INT. PUB. NIGHT

Hanson has been tied belly-down on to a table. His mouth has been
gagged and his head is bruised from the fall. Seamus and Henry are

playing darts, using his arse as a dartboard. Seamus aims, then throws his dart. It bounces off Hanson's arse. Henry smiles.

SEAMUS
(*to Henry*)
Naw, naw, that disnae count. He's tensing up his arse again.

Seamus goes over to the gagged but furious Hanson and talks in his ear.

Gonny stop tensing up yer arse? Just relax, man. It's only a game, remember.

Alistair sits nervously in a corner. Minnie is behind the bar pouring drinks.

MINNIE
(*to Alistair*)
You want anythin' son?

ALISTAIR
Ah'll huv a Caffreys, thanks.

Hanson manages to turn his head and stare disapprovingly at Alistair.

Well, Ah've no had mah staff drink, Mr Hanson.

Michael comes out of the toilet. Minnie puts his lager on the bar.

MINNIE
There's yer lager.

MICHAEL
Thanks.

The wind howls outside.

HENRY
(*to Michael*)
So where is it ye work then, son?

MICHAEL

Flemin's.

HENRY

Doon at the waterfront? Good joab?

MICHAEL

The place is full of pricks like him.

MINNIE

Whole world's full of pricks like him.

SEAMUS
(*throwing another dart*)

Mah cousin works at Flemin's.

MICHAEL

Whit's his name?

SEAMUS

Stevie Torrington.

MICHAEL

Wan-eye Torry?

SEAMUS

Ye know him?

MICHAEL

Aye.

There is a short but significant silence.

SEAMUS

Complete wank, isn't he?

MICHAEL

Ah didnae want tae say.

SEAMUS

That's aw right. Whit can ye dae? He's family, right.

MINNIE

Canny choose yer family. Whit ye're born wi' is what ye get.

Michael drinks up.

MICHAEL

Ah'm gonny head.

HENRY

Ah widnae go out in that, son. There's a gale comin'.

MINNIE

Boy's goat his work in the mornin'.

HENRY

Ye no want tae stay oan fir another wan?

MICHAEL

Naw, Ah better go.

SEAMUS
(*nodding in Hanson's direction*)
Whit dae ye think we should dae wi' him?

Michael walks across and stands looking down at Hanson.

MICHAEL

Take him out the back, take his wallet, then take a big brick each and smash them against his heid. An' don't stop till ye hear it crack open. Then turn him oan his back an' leave him tae choke oan his own blood.

Hanson looks up at Michael. He is suddenly terrified. There is a long silence.

HENRY

We couldnae dae that son.
(*to Minnie*)
Could we?

MINNIE

Ah wid never dae such a thing.

SEAMUS

Ah might if Ah wis jellied out mah nut.

MICHAEL

That's whit Ah think ye should dae. But then Ah'm the wrong person tae ask at the moment. Other than that, just take his wallet an' run like fuck.

HENRY

That's whit we'll probably dae, son. If that's aw right wi' you.

MICHAEL

Tae be honest, Ah really don't give a monkey's.

Michael walks to the door, unlocks it and goes. Henry goes over to Hanson.

HENRY

We'll just have a few more drinks, then we'll let ye go. Aw right?

Hanson nods gratefully.

INT. HIGH-RISE FLATS. NIGHT

John stands on the landing as Tanga talks to a woman who stands at her doorway. The woman goes inside and after a few moments, to John's surprise, brings a boy (aged nine) to the door. He stands there in his pyjamas as she puts on his coat, then scarf and wellies. Tanga hands over money.

INT. CAR. NIGHT

Tanga is driving. The boy sits sleepily on the back seat. John turns round every so often and smiles. The boy ignores him. The boy taps Tanga on the shoulder and Tanga pulls in. They watch as the boy walks through some wasteground and disappears round a corner. A few moments and he reappears with a small box. He jumps into the back seat and hands the box to John. John looks inside and sees the thick orange cartridges. The boy curls up in the back seat and tries to sleep.

INT. HIGH-RISE FLATS. NIGHT

John carries the sleeping boy in his arms. He knocks the door with his feet. The woman answers and matter-of-fact takes the boy from John and closes the door.

INT. CAR. NIGHT

John opens the shotgun and loads it. As he snaps it shut, any doubts he may have had are shut off also. Tanga looks at his watch.

> TANGA
> If we wait till morning' we can get him when he goes tae sign oan. Whit dae ye think?

> JOHN
> Ah think Ah'll kill him in the mornin'.

Tanga starts the car up and they drive off.

EXT. FAMILY HOME. NIGHT

Michael rings the bell. He looks through the window, etc. Realizing there's no one in, he walks away down the street.

EXT. CHAPEL. NIGHT

The rain is pouring down. Michael staggers up the steps. He pulls at the doors. They do not open. He starts banging.

INT. CHAPEL. NIGHT

Thomas hears the banging and goes to see what's happening. He shouts through the thick oak door.

> THOMAS
> Who is it?

> MICHAEL
> Thomas? Thomas, it's Michael! Let us in!

THOMAS

Michael? My brother Michael?

MICHAEL

(*almost laughing*)

Aye. Yer brother Michael. Noo let us in.

THOMAS

I can't. It's locked.

MICHAEL

Well, unlock it then?

THOMAS

I promised Father Fitzgerald I wouldn't open these doors till morning.

MICHAEL

Thomas, it's pissin' down out here. Noo Ah'm no gonny argue wi' ye. So just open the doors.

THOMAS

(*after a moment*)

No. I promised Father Fitzgerald. Do you know that vandals walked in here last month and stole the chalice. Stole it! Can you believe that?

MICHAEL

(*barely containing his anger*)

Open these fuckin' doors, Thomas.

THOMAS

No. I promised Father Fitzgerald and I'm not going to break a promise to a priest. Not for anybody. Not even for my own brother.

Michael begins to kick and shoulder the door furiously.

Why do you want in? Eh? Tell me that. Why?

MICHAEL
(*his energy dropping*)
Sanctuary, you thick, pathetic bastard. Ah want fuckin'
sanctuary.

THOMAS
No, no, no. That's not it. That's not a reason.

We hear Michael scream with rage.

Why can't you just say it? Why do you always have to be the
hard man? Why can't you just admit that you miss your
mammy and you want to be with her before they lay her to
rest. I've said it. I told Father Fitzgerald. I told him I want to
stay with my mother. I don't want her left alone here all night.
And the reason he let me stay, the reason he trusted me, was
he knew I was telling him the truth. He knew the depth of my
love for my mother. And that I was prepared to go without
sleep to be by her side. But you! You're out drinking an'
fighting and God knows whatever else. And now you want to
. . .

*A hand grabs him by the throat and pushes him up against the
door. It is Michael, soaking wet, his face white with anger.*

MICHAEL
(*as he chokes Thomas*)
You left the side door open, ya fuckin' prick. You left the side
door open! That sums you up. You set yourself up as guardian
to our mother and you go leave the fuckin' side door open!
Ah'm gonny kill you, Thomas. Ah'm gonny kill you coz
you're a fuckin' embarrassment. Ah'm ashamed to have such a
dim-witted fuck for a brother.

He lets him go.

I need a fag.

*He brings out a packet of cigarettes. He takes one out. It's soaking
wet.*

84

Fuck it! Is there a fire somewhere?

THOMAS

You can't smoke in here.

MICHAEL

Don't start me, Thomas. Don't fuckin' start me.

THOMAS

Well, if you ever came to chapel you'd know we're fully central-heated now.

MICHAEL

Aw aye. An' whit the fuck's that?

Michael points to an old-fashioned gas heater above the door.

Gie us a bunky-up.

Thomas petulantly walks across and cups his hands. Michael puts his foot in and pushes himself up. He pulls a small chain and the fire goes on. He rolls the cigarette through his fingers to let it dry.

Ah've no' done this since Ah wis an altar boy.

THOMAS

You were never an altar boy.

MICHALE

Thomas, *you* were never an altar boy. Ah wis an altar boy.

Some blood trickles down Michael's leg on to Thomas's hands. Thomas only notices this when Michael jumps down. He looks at his palms, which are bloodied, and believes it to be some kind of stigmata.

THOMAS
(*quietly*)

Michael.

He holds out his palms in a Christ-like fashion.

Fuck. It's a sign, Michael.

Michael takes a long draw from his cigarette.

MICHAEL

Aye, it's a sign, Thomas. It's a sign.

Michael walks into the chapel. He sees a half-assembled Virgin Mary.

Bloody hell, Thomas, whit have ye done?

THOMAS

It wasn't mah fault. It was Sheila.

MICHAEL

Where is Sheila?

THOMAS

She wanted to go home.

MICHAEL

Ah've just come from there. Nobody's there.

THOMAS

Well, that's where she said she was goin'.

MICHAEL

You let her leave here by herself?

THOMAS

She wanted to go.

MICHAEL

You were supposed tae be lookin' after her.

THOMAS

She didn't want me to.

MICHAEL

Well, that Ah can understand, but you were supposed tae look after her just the same.

THOMAS

Ah'm lookin' after our mother.

MICHAEL

Our mother is dead. Sheila's not.

Thomas notices blood trickling down Michael's ankles.

THOMAS

You're bleeding again.

MICHAEL
(looking down)

Aw, shit.

He takes out his shoelaces and begins tying them round his ankles.

THOMAS

That boy in the pub hurt ye, didn't he?

MICHAEL

No' as much as your fuckin' singin'. Ah'm gonny go find
Sheila. An' you better start prayin' that nothin's happened to
her.

THOMAS

Where's John?

MICHAEL

He's away tryin' tae kill a guy. But don't let that bother ye,
Thomas. As long as you're safe, that's all that matters. Right?

THOMAS

Ah love John and Sheila and you. But Ah made a promise tae
our mother an' Ah intend tae keep it.

MICHAEL

Good fir you, Thomas. Good fir useless cuntin' you.

Michael goes. Thomas returns to reassembling the Madonna.

INT. CAROLE'S HOUSE. NIGHT

*Carole and Sheila are sitting in darkness, looking out of the
window. They see a large yellow van drive up and park outside.*

88

Carole screams to her mother, who is laying the cake on a table in the centre of the room.

CAROLE

Light the candles! Light the candles! He's here!

ALISON

Right, everybody quiet. Ah don't want to hear a sound.

Her request is adhered to instantly as she begins lighting the candles. Sheila looks out of the window again, but as the father walks into the close she sees Michael walking by. She squeals. Carole instantly covers her mouth with her hand.

CAROLE

(*whispering urgently*)

Ye've goat tae keep quiet. Please, ye've goat tae or you'll ruin the surprise. Please don't. Please.

She takes her hand away. Sheila makes no further sound but watches helplessly as Michael disappears round the corner. The father comes into the room to a huge yell.

FAMILY

Surprise!

They break into a chorus of 'Happy Birthday'.

EXT. AN ALLEY BEHIND THE HANGMAN'S BAR. NIGHT

Michael is walking aimlessly when out of the darkness a gagged and bound Hanson runs into him. Hanson's expression is one of pure terror. He cowers behind Michael. Henry, Minnie and Seamus appear soon after, breathless. Seamus has a large stone in his hand. When they see how Michael glares at them, their hungry and aggressive stance soon changes to an uneasy, slightly confused guilt. Silence.

SEAMUS

Well, fuck, man, it wis your idea.

He drops the stone and runs.

MINNIE
Hey, you get back here wi' that money!

Henry and Minnie run after him. Michael takes the gag out of Hanson's mouth.

HANSON
(gabbling at ninety miles per hour)
Ah'm gonny get the polis! Ah'm gonny have yez done. The lot of yez. You'll aw dae time fir this, Ah fuckin' promise that. Ye'll aw . . .

Michael replaces the gag and picks up the stone. Hanson freezes. Then bolts. Michael drops the stone and walks off in the other direction. As he turns the corner he sees two policemen stood outside the pub door banging on it. Just as Michael makes to cross the road, there is a huge 'bang' and the side window of the police car is shattered. The policemen drop to the ground and crawl for cover. Tanga's car drives past Michael, who sees a screaming John waving a smoking shotgun at him. Michael can only stare in disbelief. Whatever energy he had suddenly seems to leave him. Everything seems to have got out of control and he is powerless to stop it. The wind howls louder and louder.

INT. CAROLE'S HOUSE. NIGHT

Darkness. Alison is lighting candles around the living room. The kids are running around.

ALISON
It's all right. It's all right. It's just a power cut.

The living-room door opens. Ed leads in Mrs Finch.

In ye come, Alice.

MRS FINCH
(*shaking*)

Ah goat such a fright. Ah wouldn't have bothered ye, but Ah'm all alone in there.

ALISON

Ah know. A storm like this gives everyone a fright. Now you just sit down and relax.

Ed helps Mrs Finch sit down. Sheila sits by the window watching. The kids have got their blankets and are laying them out on the settee.

CAROLE

Can we sleep in here the night, Ma?

ALISON

We'll see.

The doorbell rings.

ED

Bloody hell, whit is it the night?

He goes and returns shortly after with a very excited group of paper-girls.

MELISSA

My God, it's wild out there!

BERNADETTE

People are gettin' blown aboot everywhere! Where's that woman?

ALISON

That woman, as you call her, is sat right there.

BERNADETTE

Sorry, never seen ye.

ANN-MARIE

Ah brought ye yer money.

She hands Sheila the money.

MELISSA

(*to Sheila*)

Ye stayin' here the night?

ALISON

Course she is. Nobody's gaun oot in that.

BERNADETTE

We ur!

MELISSA

Man, it's brilliant oot there.

ALISON

Ed, tell them they're stayin' here till this calms doon.

ED

You tell them.

ALISON

Youse ur stayin' here.

BERNADETTE

Aye, right. See yez.

MELISSA

Bye!

ANN-MARIE

Adios.

They leave in the same hyper state as they came in. The candles are lit. Alison sits on the settee. The kids cuddle into her, covering themselves with the blankets.

CAROLE

Can we no' get a cuppa tea or anythin'?

ALISON

Ed, gonny get the wanes some juice.

ED
(having just sat down)
Listen, Ah've been workin' aw day.

ALISON
That's nice. Who went tae aw the trouble of settin' up a nice birthday party fir ye? Eh?

Ed gives in, takes a candle and goes into the kitchen. The windows rattle as the wind blows even stronger. The kids move closer to their mother and she puts both arms around them, squeezing them tightly. Alison looks up and smiles at Sheila, who smiles back. Sheila is enchanted by the image and, indeed, were she able would snuggle in too. She looks across at Mrs Finch, who seems to be having this very quiet internal conversation with herself. Sheila's gaze drops from Mrs Finch's face to her hand, upon which candle wax is dropping. Looking back to her face, she sees an old woman who is beyond feeling physical pain, such is her internal distress. Carole begins to play a tune on her mouth organ.

INT. CLOSE. NIGHT

The door of the close bangs violently open and shut. Michael is sat at the bottom of the stairs, staring into space. He looks and feels like the loneliest man on earth.

INT. CHURCH. NIGHT

Thomas holds the Madonna's head in his hands. He gently places it on to the shoulders. He stands back and smiles, well pleased with himself. Slowly he begins to hear a 'drip, drip, drip' sound and looks round to see where it might be coming from. He sees that a small puddle has developed perilously close to his mother's coffin. With a self-important, Mr DIY sigh, he empties some dry flowers from a brass vase and puts it under the offending leak. Between this and the Virgin Mary repair, he's done a good night's work. He lays his hand on the coffin.

94

THOMAS
Everythin' will be right for your service, Ma. Don't you worry.
Ah'll see tae that.

*Suddenly there is a huge 'crack' and, just as Thomas looks up to
see where it's come from, the entire roof is blown off, leaving the
chapel instantly open to the elements, which fiercely blow around
him. Thomas stands aghast. The Madonna is, once again, in pieces.
We stay on her serene, broken face as the sound of the storm
reaches its chaotic crescendo. Gradually image and sound fade to
reveal . . .*

EXT. CITY. DAY

*. . . a majestically calm sunrise over the south of the city. The huge
cranes, the old Victorian buildings, the River Clyde, even the high-
rise flats bask in its benevolent glow.*

*Only the scattered debris strewn across the empty streets suggests
the nightime mayhem. Slowly but ominously, this calm is taken
over by . . .*

EXT. STREET. DAY

*. . . two large green eyes, which, as the other image fades, we see
are those of a scrawny, vicious-looking cat sat on the bonnet of
Tanga's car staring through the windscreen. Tanga and John are
both sleeping. The gun is half hidden under a jacket on John's lap.
As we return to the cat's curious, hungry face, we dissolve slowly
to . . .*

EXT. UNDERGROUND. DAY

*. . . an underground train speeding directly towards us. Suddenly
there is a woman's scream.*

INT. UNDERGROUND TRAIN. DAY

The sound wakens Michael, who is deathly pale. He sees a small

*boy with a shoelace in his hand standing in a pool of blood which
is seeping from Michael's leg. The boy's mother dashes across and
picks him up, taking him a safe distance from Michael. The train
comes to a stop. Michael staggers to his feet and gets off, leaving
mother and son in the blood-soaked carriage.*

INT. CAROLE'S HOUSE. DAY

*Alison comes out from the toilet. She jumps back slightly as she
sees Sheila on the floor. She resists her natural instinct, which is to
bend down and help her up.*

ALISON

You all right?

SHEILA

Can I use your toilet please?

ALISON

Of course.

She steps aside. Sheila crawls into the toilet.

Ah'll just pull the door over. Ah'll no' shut it completely. An'
Ah'll stand outside, make sure the wanes don't run in on ye.
Aw right?

SHEILA
(still crawling)

Thank-you.

*Alison pulls the door over and stands in the hall. Mrs Finch comes
out of the sitting room with her zimmer.*

ALISON

Ye no' want a cup of tea or anythin', Alice?

*Mrs Finch shakes her head as she slowly makes her way to the
front door. Alison opens it for her.*

You OK now?

97

Mrs Finch nods and continues slowly out the door. Alison speaks to herself:

Christ almighty, a wee thank-you widnae kill ye, missus.

She turns and sees Louise walking sleepily into the bathroom. She dashes and manages to get her just as she pushes the door open. As she picks her up, she sees Sheila lying on the floor by the bath crying.

Louise, wait out there just now.

LOUISE

But Ah'm burstin'.

ALISON

Out. Now!

Louise goes out. Alison closes the door and locks it.

SHEILA

Ah   didn't   make   it.

ALISON

That's aw right. Don't worry about it.

SHEILA

Ah've   never   done   that   before.

ALISON

It's aw right. These things happen.

SHEILA

My   mother's   being   buried   today.

ALSION

We'll get ye changed an Ah'll take ye along, OK?

SHEILA

Ah   don't   want   to   go.

ALSION

Nobody would blame ye if ye didn't.

                         SHEILA
But   Ah   have   to   go.

                         ALISON
Ah know.

                         SHEILA
It's   terrible,   isn't   it?

                         ALISON
Let's get ye changed.

EXT. FLEMING'S FACTORY. DAY

*It's a small factory which manufactures industrial palletes. Michael
staggers in through the gates.*

INT. FLEMING'S. DAY

*Michael staggers to a large open door which looks on to the
Clyde and goes behind some machinery. He opens his shirt and
starts teasing and pulling out the blood-soaked black plastic
bags. He puts them under the machinery and, seeing his
workmates come meandering in, lets out a tired and
unconvincing yell. He takes a deep breath and stomps 'onstage',
as it were, to face his audience.*

                         MICHAEL
Bastard! How many times have Ah said that thing needed a
safety guard on it. How many times!
            (*he shows them his stab wound*)
Look at that! Fuck sake. Ye come intae yer work an' the crap
nearly kills ye!

*One of the gaffers comes walking through the crowd. Michael sees
him.*

Aye, you. It's your job tae ensure the safety in the workplace.
Well, some joab you're daen. Ah shouldnae even be here the
day, Ah'm supposed tae be at a funeral. Ah only came in coz

Ah know you're behind an' need aw the hands ye can get. An whit dae Ah get fir it? Ah nearly get killed.

Michael is running out of steam and he staggers back and forth.

Ah feel dizzy. Ah'm losin?' blood. Ah shouldnae even be here. Ah should be at a funeral. Ah'll tell ye . . . Ah want compensation . . . you're mah witnesses . . . Ah want . . . Ah want . . . Ah want mah fuckin' mammy.

With this Michael collapses backwards out of the door and lands on a discarded pallet five feet below. Before his workmates can get to him the pallet, with Michael lying on top, is floating aimlessly down the Clyde.

INT. TANGA'S CAR. DAY

Tanga and John sit waiting for Duncan down the street from his close. Connolly is playing but neither is laughing.

EXT. DUNCAN'S CLOSE. DAY

Duncan and his brother leave the close.

INT. TANGA'S CAR. DAY

TANGA
Go get him! And don't fuck up.

JOHN
Ah'll no' fuck up.

He picks up the gun and gets out of the car.

EXT. STREET. DAY

John walks very quickly towards Duncan, who has his back to him. John holds the gun up and puts his finger on the trigger.

JOHN
(*trying to sound friendly*)

Hey, PJ!

*Duncan turns and, as he does so, we see that he has a baby
strapped to his chest. John see this only at the last second and, with
his whole being geared to this moment, with an ear-piercing 'bang'
the gun goes off. For what seems like for ever nobody moves,
nobody makes a sound. Duncan looks down and the baby smiles
at him. John turns and runs, pursued by Duncan and his brother.
Tanga's passenger door remains open. As he passes, John throws
the gun into the car and carries on running.*

TANGA

Ya fuckin' shitebag!

*He quickly leans across, picks up the gun, empties out the spent
cartridges and reloads. As he looks up to see where they are,
Duncan's brother (who has run by the driver's side) stabs him in
the eye, the pain of which causes his whole body to contract,
setting the gun off. Both his legs are blown away. The car is filled
with gunsmoke and blood. Tanga sinks instantly into deep shock.*

INT. CHAPEL (OR WHAT'S LEFT OF IT). DAY

*As the various mourners come in, shocked at this roofless, soaking-
wet church, Thomas sits in the front seats looking for all the world
as if nothing's wrong. The priest speaks quietly in his ear.*

PRIEST

Ah'm very sorry, but we're not going to be able to wait for the
rest of the immediate family. The insurers are coming to
inspect the church at half-past.

THOMAS

Ye go ahead, Father.

*The priest goes, leaving Thomas in sombre/smug mode. Uncle Ian
approaches. Thomas stands up and shakes his hand.*

Thanks for comin', Uncle Ian. It's much appreciated.

UNCLE IAN

Thomas, where are they?

THOMAS

(*genuinely*)

Who?

UNCLE IAN

Your brothers and your sister.

THOMAS

Ah don't know.

UNCLE IAN

Did somethin' happen last night? Ah thought ye were aw
stayin' at yer mother's.

THOMAS

Ah stayed here last night. Just as well. If Ah hadnae been here,
mah mother could have been buried under five foot of rubble.
Have ye seen whit happened tae the statue of the Virgin
Mary? Look at that. Total write-off.

UNCLE IAN

Ah think ye should phone yer mother's. Maybe they've slept
in.

THOMAS

Man, that's sad, in't it? Ah mean, tell me whit kinda people
would sleep in fir their mother's funeral, eh? Mah own
brothers an' Sheila. She did everythin' for Sheila.

UNCLE IAN

Somethin' must've happened.

THOMAS

I'm sorry, Uncle Ian. They're mah family an' Ah love them,
but there's no excuse for not bein' here. None.

The priest begins the mass.

Ah'll see ye later.

Thomas sits down. Uncle Ian, though deeply troubled by the others' absence and Thomas's attitude, takes his seat also.

EXT. MOTORWAY. MORNING

John has managed to cross into the middle of the motorway but the traffic is too fast for him to get over to the other side. Duncan takes off his jacket, unstraps the baby and gives it to his brother, in exchange for the knife. John is watching all this closely and begins to run along the middle lane, desperately trying to find a break in the traffic. Duncan runs also, finds a break in the traffic on his side and makes it to the middle. He now stands in front of John, knife at the ready. John wraps his jacket around his arm. They jockey for position for a few moments, then come together and a fight ensues, with the traffic thundering by on either side. Somehow John manages to get the better of Duncan, gets him on the ground, takes the knife from him and puts it to his face. Duncan's brother shouts and Duncan looks up, to see him trying to cross over.

DUNCAN
(*screaming*)
Fuckin' stay where ye ur, you! Watch the fuckin' wane!

John leans across also, calms down a little, then stabs the knife into the tarmac till it breaks. He stands up, sees a break in the traffic and runs to the other side. Duncan does not pursue.

EXT. THE CLYDE. MORNING

Michael is still floating, taking in the sights – the shipyards, the new houses, the cranes, the discarded rubbish. His workmates run down alongside the embankment, unable as yet to rescue him.

INT. ALISON'S BEDROOM. DAY

Sheila sits on the bed wearing Alison's florid dressing gown. Beside her are Louise, Luke and Carole. Alison is playfully bringing out blouses and leggings from the wardrobe. Every time a garish, brightly coloured outfit is produced, Carole jumps up and down and screams excitedly.

CAROLE

That one! That one. That's beautiful.

Carole's wild enthusiasm is, as always, infectious, with the other two kids and even Sheila becoming more and more animated as regards the outfit of their choice. Sheila seems to be genuinely enjoying herself, smiling and giggling, more like a bride-to-be than a mourner at her mother's funeral. This changes suddenly when Alison produces an elegant black-silk blouse. In an instant Sheila's smile disappears.

SHEILA

That   one.

There is a moment's silence as they all stare at this simple, dark garment. As Alison studies Sheila's determined though not sorrowful face, she knows there will be no changing her mind. Carole, of course, has other ideas.

CAROLE

Aw, no' that wan! That's crap.

ALISON

That cost a fortune.

CAROLE

Ah don't care. It's horrible. It's black and it's horrible.

SHEILA
(*to Carole*)

Ah   want   it.

CAROLE

But it's horrible.

SHEILA

It's   not   horrible.

CAROLE

Ah'm tellin' ye. It is.

ALISON

Right, Carole, ye've made yer point. Now be quiet. Right,
Sheila, ye can wear it wi' these or with these. Ah can turn
them up fir ye no problem.

She holds up two pairs of silk trousers one red, one black.

CAROLE

Go for the red. Please, please, please go for the red. Ah'm
beggin' ye, please, please, please go for the red. Please. Please.

SHEILA

No.   Ah'm   gonny   go   for   the   red.

*It takes a second or two before Carole gets the joke and even then
she's more pleased about the decision than the wit. Sheila,
however, thinks it's hysterical (we thus discover yet another side to
Sheila – she loves her own jokes).*

ALISON

Right, everybody out while Sheila gets changed. Carole, run
up stairs an' see if Doreen's aw right tae look after yez for an
hour or so.

CAROLE

Aye, but Ah'm comin' wi' you two.

ALISON

Naw, ye're no'.

CAROLE

Aye, Ah um. Sheila asked me. Din't ye ask me tae come wi'
ye? Din't ye?

Sheila finds herself caught between lying and offending Carole.

> SHEILA

But it's my mother's funeral.

> CAROLE

But sure ye asked me. Din't ye?

> SHEILA
> (*unconvincingly to Alison*)

Ah did.

> CAROLE
> (*to Alison*)

There. Ah telt ye.

Carole leaves quickly before her mother can say anything. Alison knows Sheila's lying, but decides to say nothing more, respecting at least Sheila's desire not to prove her daughter a liar. Sheila tries her best to feign innocence.

EXT. STREET. MORNING

Alison, pushes Sheila, while Carole and Kimberley walk alongside. Carole still has hat and mouth organ.

> ALISON

Carole, Ah'm tellin' ye, when we get tae the chapel you take that stupid hat aff.

> CAROLE

It's no stupit.
> (*then under her breath*)

You're stupit.

Alison swipes at her.

> ALISON

What did you say there? What did you way?

> CAROLE

Nothin'.

ALISON

The church is the house of God, so you show some respect.

They turn the corner into the street facing the church. Alison doesn't notice anything as she's in full flight with Carole.

An' there is no way you're bringin' that scabby dug in. Ye tie him up outside. No havin' him sheddin' aw oer their nice . . .

She looks up at this wrecked building that was once a church.

. . . carpets.

They stare in disbelief.

CAROLE

Ah think God's gonny have tae move.

EXT. EMBANKMENT. MORNING

Michael's workmates look anxiously at the pallet, which is floating at the water's edge with no sign of Michael. They run off in different directions in search of his body.

EXT. CHURCH. MORNING

John stands looking at the debris. Somehow, he doesn't seem shocked by it. As he walks inside, Kimberley, tied to a rock, barks at him.

INT. CHURCH. MORNING

John stands unnoticed in the corridor at the back of the church. After a few moments, he takes a few steps to enter but stops himself. Though he desperately wants to go in, he feels he can't. He suddenly turns to go, but is stopped in his tracks by a grey, muddied and bloodied Michael, who stands in a little darkened alcove. Their conversation is a respectful whisper.

JOHN

Jesus.

MICHAEL

Why don't ye go in?

JOHN

Are ye aw right?

MICHAEL

Why were you gonny walk away? Why were you no' gonny go in?

John says nothing. Michael fears the worst.

Did ye kill him?

John stares at him.

Did ye kill him?

JOHN
(*finally*)

Naw.

Michael takes his brother in his arms and almost squeezes the life out of him. John begins to weep.

JOHN

Ah nearly killed him but. Nearly shot him and his baby. Ah nearly killed a baby, Michael. Whit the fuck's wrong wi' me?

MICHAEL

'Nearly' is aw right. We can live wi' nearly. Ye didne kill him or his baby. An' that's whit matters.

He sees Thomas walk up to the lectern for the reading. He looks around and sees Sheila at the front beside Alison and Carole.

See, there's Thomas and Sheila.

He turns John round so he can see them.

We made it, John. We survived the storm. Now let's join our family an' say goodbye tae wur ma wi' the grace that she deserves.

III

They go inside, Michael's arm around John. The congregation's heads turn as they walk down the aisle. Thomas sees them both but carries on with the reading. Michael whispers:

You know the one thing that really saddens me about aw this?
> (*he stares at Thomas*)

That Ah've fucked up more than any of us.

He collapses immediately.

JOHN
> (*to congregation*)

Gie us a haun here!

Uncle Ian and others go to his aid.

SHEILA

Michael!

UNCLE IAN

Put him in mah motor an' we'll get him tae hospital. Now!

They pick him up and begin carrying him out.

SHEILA

John!   John!

John runs over to his sister.

Ah   want   tae   go   with   Michael.

John pushes Sheila, both looking to Thomas, who has remained speechless at the lectern. John stops just in front of him.

JOHN

You comin'?

Thomas can only respond with a blank, bewildered expression. John knows no other answer will be forthcoming and rushes up the aisle with Sheila. Thomas takes control of himself and

continues the reading.

EXT. CEMETERY. DAY

The hearse and the mourners gather by the graveside. The undertakers open the back of the hearse and begin sliding out the coffin. Thomas steps forward.

                    THOMAS
Ah'll take her.

                    UNDERTAKER
You'll need some help, sir.

                    THOMAS
Ah said Ah'll take her. On my own.

                    UNDERTAKER
I'm sorry, sir, I think you'll find she's too heavy.

                    THOMAS
              (*without a hint of irony*)
She ain't heavy. She's my mother.

The undertaker has no reply to this. Thomas, to the utter bewilderment of the mourners, puts his back under the coffin and walks with it on his back. Needless to say, he gets about four feet before the weight flattens him into the mud. The undertaker sighs and signals to his partner and others to get the coffin off him.

INT. KITCHEN. DAY

It's a very similar set-up to before, when the family awaited their mother's arrival. Uncle Ian is there, with John and Sheila. There is little conversation, just drinking of tea and eating of biscuits.

INT. FLOWER SHOP. DAY

An efficient and somewhat chirpy Thomas is handed a wreath by

the shop assistant. He still bears a scar on his nose from his previous fall.

INT. KITCHEN. DAY

John comes into the kitchen.

> JOHN
>
> Michael's here.

He leaves, followed immediately by Ian and Sheila. They go through the hall to the front door, where a gaunt but very much alive Michael stands, flanked by two paramedics. He smiles broadly.

EXT. CEMETERY. DAY

Thomas lays the wreath by his mother's headstone. He removes a few leaves from the grave then sits down beside it. He looks around, then brings out a quarter-bottle of whisky from his pocket and drinks some. He sits looking over his surroundings as if expecting something to happen. Nothing does. Nothing will.

Thomas is working at the graveside.

> MICHAEL
> (*out of view*)
>
> Aw right, Thomas?

Thomas turns and there stand Michael, John and Sheila.

> THOMAS
>
> When did ye get oot the hospital?

> MICHAEL
>
> About an hour ago.

> THOMAS
>
> Nobody telt me.

JOHN

Ah telt ye.

THOMAS

When?

JOHN

Last night.

THOMAS

Naw ye never.

JOHN

Aye, Ah did. Ah telt ye Michael wis getting' oot the hospital this morning' an' we were gonny pick him up. An' wid you want to come wi' us?

THOMAS

Nuh, no way. Ah'd remember that.

SHEILA

Ah telt ye inaw.

THOMAS

When?

SHEILA

Last night.

THOMAS
(to Michael)

Nobody telt me. Ah'd remember.

MICHAEL

It's aw right. Don't worry about it.

THOMAS

Ah'm no' worried about it. Nobody telt me. Ah'd have remembered.

There is a brief and awkward silence.

Ah wis gonny come an' visit ye, but Ah've been kinda
busy.

MICHAEL
(*looking at the grave*)
Ah can see that.

THOMAS
Yer lookin' well though

MICHAEL
Ah look like shite.

THOMAS
Naw, naw, naw. Ye're lookin' very fit. Ye lost weight?

MICHAEL
About four and a half pints' worth.

THOMAS
Aye, coz yer face is lookin' very sharp. Good strong jawline.

MICHAEL
Thanks.

THOMAS
Naw, nae problem. Lookin' good, brother.

*There is another brief pause. Michael studies the grave,
momentarily lost in his own private thoughts.*

MICHAEL
See ye, Ma. Right, Ah'm gonny head before Ah starts greetin'
again.
(*to Thomas*)
We're gonny go for an Indian. Ye comin'?

THOMAS
Ach. Dunno.

MICHAEL

C'mon.

THOMAS

Dunno.

MICHAEL

Well, ye're invited.

THOMAS

Thanks fir that. Ah might see yez doon there later. Where yez gaun?

MICHAEL

Shannands.

THOMAS

Aye, well Ah might see yez there.

MICHAEL

You're no gonny come, ur ye?

Thomas says nothing.

Ah just want ye tae know we're here for ye. Ah just wanted ye tae know that.

THOMAS

Ah know that. An' Ah'm here for youse.

MICHAEL

Naw, ye're no' here for us. The place is full of deid people, Thomas. We don't belong here. Now, ur ye comin?

THOMAS

Ah'm no' really hungry.

MICHAEL
(*to John and Sheila*)

Let's go.

*They walk away purposefully. Thomas is left deeply
uncomfortable. He shouts after them.*

THOMAS
But Ah meant it when Ah said Ah wis here fir yez. No' here as
in bloody here as in a cemetery, but as in here, in mah heart
sorta thing.

*They keep walking. He watches after them, caught somewhere
between staying and going. He shouts:*

Ah could maybe come just for a starter. Their mushroom
pakora's good.

*They continue walking without turning round. He begins walking,
then running towards them. When he catches up they walk only a
few paces before he suddenly turns and begins to run back. He
stops at the grave.*

See ye, Ma. See ye, Da. God bless.

He runs back after the others. We stay on the gravestone.

Fade.

Credits

Written and Directed by Peter Mullan
Produced by Frances Higson
Executive Producer Paddy Higson
Director of Photography Grant Scott Cameron
Music composed by Craig Armstrong
Film Editor Colin Monie
Designer Campbell Gordon
Costume Designer Lynn Aitken
Make-up Designer Anastasia Shirley

CAST

MICHAEL	Douglas Henshall
THOMAS	Gary Lewis
SHEILA	Rosemarie Stevenson
JOHN	Stephen McCole
MOTHER OF FAMILY	Ann Swan
FRANK	Gilbert Martin
SANDRA (Woman in Bar)	Jan Wilson
JULIAN (Bar Manager)	Lenny Mullan
DUNCAN	Malcolm Shields
MONA	June Brogan
LENNY (Duncan's brother)	Paul Doonan
EVELYN (Waitress in Bar)	Linda Cuthbert
LEX KEITH	As Himself
HUGH FERRIS	As Himself
NEIL (Lad in Toilet)	Joel Strachan
ALISTAIR (Taxi Driver)	Tam White
MARIA (Receptionist at Evette's)	Vanya Eadie
MARGARET	Dorothy Jane Stewart
RAB (Cheeky Boy in Street)	Michael Mallon
PEACHY (Cheeky Boy in Street)	James Casey
JAMES (Cheeky Boy in Street)	Alan Gracie
LIAM (Bus Driver)	Jim Twaddale

TANGA	Frank Gallagher
MR BELL	Eric Barlow
MRS BELL	Frances Carrigan
AMANDA (Baby-sitter)	Judith A. Williams
DAVID (Michael's Son)	Michael Sharpe
CAROLE	Laura O'Donnell
ANN MARIE (Paper-girl)	Lee-Ann McCran
MELISSA (Paper-girl)	Debbie Welsh
BERNADETTE (Paper-girl)	Donna Chalmer
LOUISE (Carole's Sister)	Sarah Hepburn
ALISON (Carole's Mum)	Deirdre Davis
MRS FINCH	Sheila Donald
ALICE	Martha Leishman
ANGELA (Michael's Daughter)	Catherine Connell
ED (Carole's Dad)	John Commeford
ALISTAIR (Barman in Pub)	Stephen Docherty
HANSON	Alex Norton
MOIRA (Woman Collecting)	Louise Dunn
PAPER BOY (In Pub)	Luke Coulter
HENRY (In Basement)	Laurie Ventry
MINNIE (In Basement)	Maureen Carr
SEAMUS (In Basement)	Steven Singleton
DEAF BOY'S MUM	Kate Brailsford
FRASER (Deaf Boy)	Luka Kennedy
JESSICA (Woman in Tube)	Helen Devon
DUNCAN'S BABY	Josie Aitken Sheridan
FATHER FITZGERALD	Seamus Ball
UNCLE IAN	Dave Anderson
MR LEITCH (Undertaker)	Robert Carr
AUNT GERALDINE	Jenny Swan

CREW

Casting Director	Doreen Jones
Casting Assistant	Lenny Mullan
1st Assistant Director	Mark Goddard
2nd Assistant Director	Guy Heeley
3rd Assistant Director	Mike Queen
Floor Runner	Mark Murdoch
Script Supervisor	Janis Watt

Continuity Trainee	Karen Wood
Production Manager	Martell
Production Coordinator	Gillian Berrie
Production Assistant	Jessica Rundle
Production Runner	Jenny Williams
Assistant to the Company	Emma Davie
Location Manager	John Booth
Location Assistants	Michael Higson
	Robert Etherson
Production Accountant	Louise Coulter
Assistant Accountant	John McKain
Trainee Accountant	Neil Cairns
Wardrobe Supervisor	Margie Fortune
Wardrobe Assistant	Carole Millar
Make-up Assistants	Sarah Kramer
	Claire Davies
Sound Recordist	Peter Brill
Boom Operator	Peter Murphy
Sound Trainee	Alastair Mason
Focus Pullers	Jonathan Sykes
	Francis Todd
Clapper Loarder	Kirstin McMahon
Camera Car Driver	Clive Tocher
Camera Trainee	Joe Gormley
Steadicam Operator	John Ward
Grips	Eddie Burt
	Stuart Bunting
Gaffer	Mark Ritchie
Best Boy	Paul McGeachan
Electricians	John Adamson
	Fraser Campbell
Generator Operator	Gary Thompson

2ND UNIT

Camera Operator	Oliver Cheeseman
Focus Puller	Alan McSheehy
Focus Operator	Andrew Ford
Focus Pullers	Chris Burns
	Kathy Friend

Assistant Directors	Ted Mitchell
	Neil Smith
Art Director	Frances Connell
Assistant Art Director	Cliona Harkin
Art Department Assistant	Caroline Grebbell
Story-Board Artist	Alan Reid
Prop Master	David Reilly
Prop Buyer	Mike Ireland
Dressing Props	Jim Davers
Stand-by Props	Scott Keery
	Tony Sheridan
Construction Manager	Danny Sumsion
Carpenter	Alex Robertson
Painter	Paul Curran
Stagehand	Mark Brady
Stand-by Carpenter	Chris Higson
Stand-by Stagehand	William Maxwell
Stand-by Rigger	Billy Wilson
Rigger Nightshoots	Tony Richards
1st Assistant Editor	David Gibson
2nd Assistant Editor	Lorraine Keiller
3rd Assistant Editor	Giles Burgess
Supervising Dubbing Editor	Hilary Wyatt
Dialogue Editor	Lorraine Keiller
Dubbing Mixer	Pat Hayes
Assistant Dubbing Mixer	John Fitzgerald
Foley recordist	Ted Swanscott
Foley Artists	Lionel Selwyn
	Felicity Cotterell
ADR mixer	Mike Prestwood Smith
Additional ADR	Bronek Korda
Special Effects Supervisor	Stuart Brisdon
Special Effects Operators	Mark Haddenham
	Mike Tilley
	Colin Tilley
	Nick Cooper
Visual and Model Effects	Roy Field, BSC
Matte and Scenic Artist	Cliff Culley
Model Cameraman	Neil Culley

Model Construction	Steve Corduroy
Optical Printer	Dick Dimbleby
Stunt Coordinator	Nick Powell
Assistant Stunt Coordinators	Stuart Clark
	Steve Griffin
Stunt Performers	Daniella DaCosta
	Nrinder Dhudwar
	Ray Nicholas
	Nick Wilkinson
Armourer	Bernard Shepherd
Unit Publicist	Shirley Whiteside
Stills Photographer	Alan Wylie
Stand-ins	Emma Olver
	Paul Shirley
Unit Drivers	Jas Brown
	Danny Mitchell
Artist Winnebago	Colin King
Chaperones	Anne Marie Coulter
	Lucy Kennedy
	Anne Sharpe
Carer to Rosemarie Stevenson	Annette Stevenson

SCREEN FACILITIES GROUP
Carl Whitehouse, Jim Wyse, Dave Anforth, Tony Boucher

THISTLE CATERING
Brendan Diver, Tom Gibb, Charlie Duffy,
Nicky, Tom Urquhart

MEDICAL SUPPORT
British Red Cross, Stars,
Buckingham Back Clinic, Splashsports

Religious Technical Adviser	Rev. Vincent Perricone
Rostrum Camera	Malcolm Paris
Title Artwork	Blue Peach
Opticals	GSE-Mick Lennie
Negative Cutting	Sylvia Wheelers
Orchestra	The BT Scottish Ensemble

127

Music Programmer	Richard T. Norris
Music Supervisor	Sandy Dworniak
Orchestra Contractor	Roger Pollen
Music Assistant	Sarah Dolan
Music Engineer	Paul Hulme

SOUNDTRACK

Billy Connolly – Solo Concert
'Marie's Wedding', 'The Jobby Wheecha!!!', 'The Crucifixion'
All written and performed by Billy Connolly,
Courtesy of Sleepy Dumpling Music

SONGS

'Ye Can Come and See the Baby'
Written by Will Fyffe
Performed by Hugh Ferris & Lex Keith
Courtesy of Francis Day & Hunter Ltd

'Going Doon The Water'
by Neil Grant & Andy Stewart
Performed by Hugh Ferris & Lex Keith
Courtesy of Lochside Music Publishing

'The Air That I Breathe'
by Mike Hazlewood/Albert Hammond
Performed by Gary Lewis
Courtesy of EMI April Music/Rondor Music

'You Take the High Road'
Performed by Hugh Ferris & Lex Keith

'Bean-Bag' (Fairground Music)
Composed and Arranged by Shandy and Dave
Courtesy of Test Industries

Sound Design by	Reelworks
Foley recorded at	De Lane Lea
ADR recorded at	Goldcrest Studios
Music recorded at	Air Edel Studios
Film Laboratories	Rank Film Laboratories
Camera Equipment & Film Stock	Sammy's
Lighting Equipment	Lee Lighting
Sound Equipment	Brill Sound
Grip Equipment	Grip House North
Cherry Pickers & Cranes	Brogan Access

Film Editing Equipment	Edithire
Car Hire	Arnold Clark
Truck Hire	Turner Hire Drive
Action Vehicles	Brian Morrison
Security	Forgewood Security
Insurance	Aon Ruben – David Havard
Lawyer	S. J. Berwin – Jacqueline Hurt
Completion Bond	Film Finance Services Ltd
Dubbing Studios	Ardmore Sound

*Antonine Green Bridge would like to thank the following
for their support in the making of this film:*

George Thompson, CAVA studios, Kay Sheridan,
Denise Gibson, Anne Coulter, Anne, Mairi & Patrick Swan,
Paul McManus, Kate Leys, Eddie Dick,
St Johns Reform School, All Saints Episcopal Church,
SCET, Glasgow Film Theatre, Crosshill Parish Church,
Jim Irvine, MCPS, Mike Alexander – Pelicula Films, Dave Read,
John Gow, Glasgow Film Office, Kevin Kane,
Albert Gonella, Billy Connolly

Mixed in
Dolby Digital Surround Sound
at
Ardmore Studios, Bray, Ireland.

Edited on film
Filmed entirely on location in Glasgow, Scotland.
Development funded by The Scottish Film Production Fund.

An Antonine Green Bridge Production
for
The Glasgow Film Fund
and
Channel 4